PRAISE FROM WORLD BUSINESS LEADERS FOR

Asia for Women on Business

"As a Chinese woman who grew up in Asia, I found the Wilens' book to be an accurate portrayal of how men and women interact in the Asian business world. . . . Extremely readable, filled with anecdotes, tips, and pointers."

> Lin L. Chan, Corporate Controller, Sola International, Inc.

"Having a good business idea is only half the equation—the more important half is getting it to be heard. *Asia for Women on Business* delivers the tools you need to be heard as a respected businesswoman in Asia."

> Mona L. Sabuco, Analyst, Management Reporting and
> Analysis, Chevron Research and Technology Company

"This book is as essential for women working in Asia as having the right telephone connectors for their notebook computers! They should give it to their managers *and* team members. . . . By walking us through examples, the authors let us experience what might happen and how we can learn to respond appropriately."

> Deborah Satten, Pacific Product Marketing Manager,
> Apple Computer, Inc.

"The Wilens offer their male reader the chance to experience essential business issues and situations with a perspective rarely provided. The text offers more than reference material; it examines real-life business experiences and heightens awareness of critical issues."

> Jim L. Apfel, Senior Sales Manager, Diamond Multimedia
> Systems, Inc.

"This is a book that anyone traveling to Asia should read."

> Charles Chua, American Express Travel

HONG KONG

TAIWAN

SINGAPORE

SOUTH KOREA

ASIA

for Women on Business

Tracey Wilen & Patricia Wilen

Stone Bridge Press
Berkeley, California

Published by STONE BRIDGE PRESS
P.O. Box 8208 • Berkeley, California 94707
TEL 510-524-8732 • FAX 510-524-8711

Printed in the United States of America.

10 9 8 7 6 5 4 3 2 1

Library of Congress Cataloging-in-Publication Data

Wilen, Tracey.
　　Asia for women on business : Hong Kong, Taiwan, Singapore, South
Korea / Tracey Wilen & Patricia Wilen.
　　　　p.　　cm.
　　Includes bibliographical references and index.
　　ISBN 1-880656-17-5
　　1. Women in business—Asia.　2. Corporate culture—Asia.　3. Women
in business—Travel—Asia.　I. Wilen, Patricia.　II. Title.
HD6181.85.W55　　1995
650.1'082—dc20
　　　　　　　　　　　　　　　　　　　　　　　　　　　95-20670
　　　　　　　　　　　　　　　　　　　　　　　　　　　CIP

Dedication

To my father—
Thanks for being a role model, a mentor, a father, and a friend

TRACEY WILEN

To my husband, Art—
For his lifelong patience, support, encouragement, and love

To my daughter, Tracey—
who constantly amazes me with her wit, charm, and *joie de vivre*

PATRICIA D. WILEN

Contents

Introduction

Asia is moving into the future with amazing speed and skill, and today presents a real challenge to the West. A previous book coauthor Tracey Wilen worked on, *Doing Business with Japanese Men*, was written from a women's perspective and focused on Asia's leading economic power- house. So positive was the response to that book and so numerous were the requests from women for information on doing business elsewhere in Asia that we decided to create a new handbook, this time about the next tier of leading-edge Asian economies, the so-called Four Tigers of Hong Kong, Taiwan, Singapore, and South Korea. (Mainland China and other Asian countries like the Philippines, Indonesia, Vietnam, and Thailand are not yet in the same league but are coming up fast.)

The Four Tigers, over the last few decades, have developed sophisti- cated manufacturing infrastructures to keep a multitude of finished prod- ucts rolling off the assembly lines for export abroad. The United States has encouraged their growth by welcoming the cheaper Asian products into America without demanding reciprocity, and through aid, as in the cases of Taiwan and South Korea. Strong leaders allowed the Four Tigers, until only recently, to concentrate political power on economic growth. Cheap labor has helped them remain competitive. Now, in keeping with the information age, Asia's well-educated work forces are stimulating the development of new technologies. All count the United States as their top trading partner and foreign investor, or among the top three.

America and the Four Tigers have, in fact, become codependent. Without the availability of attractive, inexpensive Asian goods, the U.S.

standard of living would suffer. Without the huge American market in which to sell their goods, Asia's economy would falter. It is therefore essential that we understand our trading partners and that they understand us.

Many Western women are now traveling back and forth to do business in the Four Tigers. Few, however, understand Asian traditions, customs, and behavior. Even fewer seem to recognize the importance of following Asian protocol to ensure the success of their business dealings.

As a Western women you should be aware that in Asia you will find yourself in societies where traditionally a woman's predominant role has been to manage the household and serve her family (perhaps after a short stint in the business world as a clerk or secretary). The same Confucian principles that gave Asia, in the opinion of many analysts, its high regard for diligence, etiquette, and devotion also taught that each person had his or her place in society and served society best by living up to society's expectations. As a woman doing business, therefore, you are in Asian terms a person somewhat "out of place." As a *Westerner* you are of course not expected to conform to Asian cultural standards, and yet as a *person* doing business in Asia you are expected to form close human relationships with your partners.

It is still difficult for many Asian men to make the leap where you become both a business partner *and* a woman. How you deal with this situation depends on several different things: how much it bothers you, how flexible you judge your Asian counterpart to be, how much the deal is worth, and so on. Asian men born before 1950 still retain many of the traditional attitudes, whereas men born later tend to be much more receptive to women in business (and may have spent considerable time overseas honing their cultural and language skills). In general you will have the most difficulties in Korea and Japan. But don't assume that every Asian businessman is waiting for you to prove your competence. Nor should you be unaware of the very real problems you may face—it is best to be prepared.

We hope this book will give you a competitive edge by introducing you to these four Asian cultures through their background and their important similarities and differences. All information here is geared toward a woman's view of Asia in terms of what to expect and how to deal with your Asian business counterparts. We have emphasized not only your role as a businesswoman in Asia, but also the role of women in these societies and how this will affect you in all aspects of your business, from representing your company in a management position to closing a sale. We have included helpful hints on cultural differences and how to handle the necessary social protocol. We have also included information on how to educate your coworkers and Asian counterparts on women in business while presenting yourself in the best possible light.

Chapters 1–3 are overviews of all Four Tigers as a group, from the standpoints of dealing with culture shock when you first arrive, doing business, and handling after-hours entertainment. Chapter 4 examines the problems of gender discrimination and sexual harassment and offers strategies for dealing with them. Chapter 5 shows you how to apply your newly learned Asian social skills while dining—which is a big part of doing business in Asia. Chapters 6 through 9 treat each country individually, exploring general etiquette and business practices in more detail.

Included in these later chapters is information on matters of particular importance to women. All hotels listed were recommended to us by traveling businesswomen for their services, security, and comfort. All, for example, have a full range of business services, from translation services to business centers, secretarial services, and business equipment. They provide in-room amenities such as minibars and toiletries, and they offer room service and dining facilities suitable for all occasions. All accept major credit cards. Although these hotels are fairly expensive, companies can usually obtain frequent-use discounts. The restaurants included here were similarly recommended to us as being excellent venues for dining with clients or places that offer familiar Western foods where you can dine alone in comfort. And although our primary focus is on your business needs, we have also listed things to see and do, good buys, and great places to shop, as well as background information on each country that will help prepare you for your trip. You will of course find more extensive accommodation, dining, and travel listings in conventional travel guidebooks or, after your arrival, at your hotel's information desk.

The four country chapters follow identical formats; individual treatments vary, however, reflecting differences among the countries as well as what they offer—or fail to offer—the Western woman traveling alone. The chapter on Singapore includes more extensive nightlife recommendations than the other chapters, because Singapore has many places where you will feel comfortable and because of its well-deserved reputation for personal safety.

At the end of the book are three Appendixes. The first gives you pointers for making business presentations in the Four Tigers, the second suggests ways you can ensure your safety while traveling, and the third is a detailed guide to golf courses (which we believe is a first for a business guide to Asia).

To bring in some first-hand knowledge, we have included insights from interviews we conducted with businesspeople who have either traveled to Asia or worked for an Asian company in the United States or abroad. We especially sought out women who had work experience in several different countries. Their individual accounts present personal views on various aspects of the Four Tigers and some thoughts on the intricacies of doing business in Asia.

Despite our efforts to include all necessary information, what we have provided is only fragmentary at best. Also, in a book like this it is impossible to avoid generalizations that may not apply to particular individuals or situations. Keeping these points in mind, you should err on the side of caution. Dress conservatively and, when in doubt, observe and follow your Asian counterparts, or just use your most conservative Western business etiquette. Careful observation and caution should get you through almost any situation gracefully. At the same time, remember that your Asian counterparts appreciate the same qualities that you do—attention to detail, respect, and sincerity.

While we were gathering information for this book, we asked an Asian friend to sum up the differences between the Four Tigers. She commented that if she were to describe each culture from its own point of view, she would say that Hong Kong sees itself as the center of the world; Taiwan sees itself as the main supplier of the world's goods today; South Korea plans to overtake the competition to become the main supplier tomorrow; and Singapore thinks its role is to placate the world and set a moral standard. Yet when Asians talk about how they view each other, the perspective changes: Asians rate Koreans as the most emotional, Taiwanese as the most flexible, Singaporeans as the most trustworthy, and Hong Kong Chinese as driven by short-term thinking.

All this is obviously a great oversimplification. But it does suggest how the nature of Asia today is hardly monolithic and demands careful study. Since the format of this book is built around lists of tips and pointers, you can easily skip around to find discussions that relate to your specific needs. We do recommend, however, that you read Chapters 2, 3, and 5 carefully, as they will help ground you in many aspects of common Asian business practices.

No matter how you choose to use this book, we hope its guidelines will help you succeed in your business ventures—and enjoy your trip as well.

Note on Romanization

Words in the native languages of the countries featured in this book appear in letters of the English alphabet according to conventions followed by the respective governments and travel agencies. We have tried to present place names in the forms and spellings you will most likely encounter in maps and guidebooks. In most cases, these romanizations accurately represent the pronunciations of the words, but not always. The biggest problems involve Chinese. The *pinyin* method of romanization introduced in the 1950s by mainland China is favored by most modern linguists, but it has not been fully adopted in Taiwan and Hong Kong. In those places you will find many Chinese words romanized according to the older Wade-Giles system; also some common spellings of Chinese words and place names are "easy" spellings adopted over the years by non-native speakers. Since there is no single, consistent solution here, we have decided to follow our native guides and to advise you to be prepared for the spellings in this book to now and then not match what you will see printed elsewhere or while traveling. In a few cases, we have provided both *pinyin* and Wade-Giles renderings of Chinese business terms known primarily in the West in their *pinyin* forms.

Acknowledgments

The authors would like to thank the numerous businesspeople and organizations that helped us collect data for this book, provided personal contacts, and shared their experience and advice. We would especially like to thank our friends and colleagues at:

ALZA Pharmaceuticals
American Association of University Women
American Express Travel
Apple Computer
Automation Group
Chevron
Cisco Systems
Consulate General of Singapore
Consulate General of the Republic of Korea
Aaron D. Cushman and Associates
Deputy United States Trade Representative

Diamond Multimedia Systems
East West Center
Embassy of the Republic of Korea, Consular Section
Equal Employment Opportunity Commission
Far East Trade Service (ROC)
Gent and Associates
Goldstar Electronics (LG Electronics)
Hewlett-Packard
Hong Kong Economic and Trade Office
Hong Kong Trade Development Council
Hyundai Electronics
Jade Systems
Orbyx Global Trade Group
Pepsico
Samsung Electronics
Singapore Tourist Promotion Board
Sola International
Stanford University
Sun Microsystems

1 | Culture Shock

Whenever I travel to a new country in Asia, the feeling is the same. I get off the plane and feel overwhelmed by the crowds. I realize now that we have a lot more personal space in our country than others do. The next thing I notice is that most countries are more polluted and unsanitary, so I don't want to touch anything for fear of getting sick. These countries are industrial, gray, and under constant construction, so there is a lot of rubble and dirt. The first day in Asia is always tough for me. I arrive in the late afternoon. I try to force myself to get outside and walk around, even for an hour. Inside, I just want to take a hot shower or bath and crawl into bed. It's difficult to walk around outside because I can't read the street signs and all the buildings seem to look the same. Anyway, I usually can get around the block and into a store or two. I always feel like people are staring at me because I'm walking around alone and unescorted. I do better now compared to my first trips. I recall getting into some countries on a Saturday and not leaving my room until I had to on Monday morning. (San Diego, California)

Most Westerners visiting Asia for the first time experience culture shock. Suddenly being thrust into a culture that has different customs and values can create severe distress. This is especially true when you have to adjust and respond to different cultural cues. You may feel overwhelmed when you visit Asia not only because of the unfamiliar languages, crowds, and noise, but also because of the differences in male/female roles. You may experience a variety of emotions including isolation, anxiety, and depression, and you may often feel intimidated. If you remain in this new environment for a long period of time, you may also experience a sense of being cut off, and this can lead to severe homesickness. In our interviews with our business peers traveling to Asia, we were frequently exposed to their culture-shock reactions, reminding us of our own initial responses to the Asian environment.

Our interviews indicate that culture shock may often be more severe for women. As a businesswoman traveling to Asia, you may not meet other women in the business environment, except those in significantly lower ranking support roles. It may be difficult for you to find a female confidant during your stay. You may also feel distress from having to dine and travel alone. You will be stared at, which can add to your discomfort.

It is natural to want to avoid uncomfortable situations. But remember that you are in Asia on important business as a representative of your firm. Culture shock is a very real experience, and you need to be aware of any negative feelings that might interfere with your business transactions and your ability to act naturally and confidently.

Culture shock can be reduced if you can share your experiences with others or if you can discover some recognizable overlaps with Western culture to which you can respond naturally. By making a conscious effort you should be able to keep your balance during your stay in Asia. Remember, most people adjust well to new cultures and enjoy their new experiences. Being well prepared will help you feel good about where you are going and the people you are meeting. This, in turn, will help ensure the success of your business venture.

WHAT WOMEN SAY

Checking In
Whenever we go to Asia for business, we tend to call each other after we arrive, while if we are doing business in the U.S., we may not meet until the morning of the first meeting. Many times I get in and call someone in the middle of the day. If it is their first trip, they may be sleeping. Sure, it could be jet lag, but more often than not I suspect it is culture shock and they are trying to escape it by sleeping. (Boston, Massachusetts)

Excuse Me!

An odd thing I noticed in Singapore is the lack of pedestrian protocol. In the U.S. we walk to the right. In Singapore they walk where they please and bump into people a lot. When my colleague came over to the U.S. I had to show him how to walk politely here since his walking pattern would be considered very rude. (Morristown, New Jersey)

Helping Hand

I met a woman in Taiwan who was perhaps more westernized than others because she worked for a jointly owned Eastern/Western firm. She wanted to practice her English, so she spent a lot of time taking me around Taiwan. I learned how to appreciate the good things and overlook the dirt. It helped me get over my initial gut-wrenching feelings about Taiwan. I think it is good to get to know the people there because they are very warm. (Chicago, Illinois)

Rude Help

A Korean man from whom I had politely asked directions at a train station angrily yelled his response at me and walked away. I was shocked but said nothing. A few minutes later, the same man saw me getting on the wrong train, stopped me, directed me to the right train, boarded it with me, and finally told me where to get off. All the while he spoke in an angry voice, frowned, and kept his eyes averted. I felt humiliated and bewildered. (Singapore)

Where Do We Go from Here?

The first time I went to Taiwan was only for two days. It was overwhelming for me. I recall getting in at night and walking around the streets with some of my colleagues. We all were feeling pretty awkward. We saw so many roaches and water beetles it was hard not to lose our appetites. We did not feel good about any local restaurant we saw and went back to the hotel. All I would eat was rice and a can of Coke. (San Ramon, California)

Wilted

Singapore was not what I expected. It's a beautiful city. The only drawback was the heat and humidity. The weather in Singapore leaves you nonfunctional until you adjust. You will always be hot in Singapore. That was difficult to deal with. (London, England)

Pushy Salesman
In a Korean market, this man came up and pushed a purse into my hand.
I kept saying no, thank you, but he kept pushing it into my hand. I knew
he wanted me to buy it. I kept walking down the street and pushing him
away and became very exasperated. Business associates later told me
that if I had taken it from him, it would mean I wanted to buy it and I
would never get rid of him. (Akron, Ohio)

At Home with the Roaches
I was sent to Singapore as an expatriate. They treat you very well and
you live in a very nice ex-pat complex removed from mainstream society.
Anyway, the first place I was put while waiting for my place to get
cleaned was horrendous. It was roach infested and gross. (Portland, Oregon)

Island Fever
After I had been in Singapore for a few days, I realized that I had seen
everything there was to see. Fortunately, I bumped into some expatriates. They said I was experiencing "island fever" since Singapore has
only a limited number of things to do. The best solution, they said, is to
travel. They advised me to start taking a few four-day weekends and go
somewhere else like Malaysia or Thailand. I had to spend eight weeks in
Singapore, and it was a big adjustment. (Armonk, New York)

It's a Man's World
You can see the difference in how women are treated in Taiwan, Singapore, and Hong Kong over Korea and Japan. It really bothers me as a
Western male with three kids, one a daughter, to see women today kneeling to men in the bars in Korea and Japan. It is not how I want my
daughter to be raised. (Fremont, California)

DIFFERENCES TO WATCH FOR

Differences abound. Here are some of the more obvious.

➤ *Crowds*
   If you are going to shop or use public transportation in the Four

Tigers, be prepared to be locked into masses of people and shoved on occasion without an apology. Traditionally, Asians pay little heed to anyone outside their family, work unit, or friends. Because they have no established relationship with outsiders, they are not obligated to show concern for them.

➤ *Pollution*
Singapore is very clean, but the other Tigers are polluted with construction debris and dust, factory effluvia, and exhaust fumes from heavy traffic. City streets may seem dingy and littered. Noise, particularly from mopeds and construction equipment, can be deafening.

➤ *Vermin*
Every city has its share of roaches and rats, some more than others.

➤ *Traffic*
Modern traffic on roads built for rickshaws and carts and exploding populations running amuck on mopeds contribute to a commuting nightmare.

➤ *Unpleasant Weather*
The heat and humidity in all Four Tigers can be overwhelming in the summer, while the cold and dampness of Korea in winter can be equally difficult. The monsoon season comes during the hottest time of the year, and it may rain and steam for days on end.

➤ *Bargaining*
Most Westerners are not used to haggling and feel uncomfortable doing it. Nonetheless, bring your street smarts, since bargaining is accepted practice in Asia, except at department stores and hotel shops, which have fixed prices.

➤ *Gender Discrimination*
Women are generally not treated with the same deference as men, and Western women find this particularly hard to deal with.

➤ *Strange Food*
You may feel uncomfortable with the choices of food offered and the dubious sanitation, and you may have no idea how to order a meal. If your stomach feels uneasy about venturing in new culinary directions, stick to hotel coffee shops or Western fast-food eateries. (See also Chapter 5 and individual country chapters.)

FEELINGS YOU MAY HAVE

➤ *Depressed*

When you have to deal with great multitudes of people speaking a foreign tongue and with vastly different customs and lifestyles, it is easy to become anxious and irritable. The resulting feeling of being helpless to do anything about your situation can lead to depression and an overall loss of energy.

➤ *Disoriented*

You will be in countries where English is not used on street signs, office buildings, or restaurants. Panic can set in quickly. It is not only very frustrating to try to find your way in an unfamiliar environment, but it can also be frightening when you don't recognize where you are and realize that you can't just ask anyone to help you out.

➤ *Intimidated*

Most of us like to feel that we are well organized and in control of our environment. In Asia, however, you may feel frustrated and thwarted by the numerous steps it may take to do a simple task.

➤ *Alienated*

When you travel abroad, you will feel foreign and out of place, particularly if you don't speak the language. In Asia it is not likely that you will be invited to join a social group or even be approached at a party to dance. You will more likely be left on your own, which may cause you to feel rejected and uncertain about how to proceed.

➤ *Bored*

Because of language difficulties, there are not many places you can easily visit in the evenings or on weekends. Since you don't know too many people, you can't even make phone calls to lessen your isolation. Sightseeing presents both transportation and language problems as do sojourns to the movies and theater—but how many times can you watch the same CNN or Sky Net programs?

➤ *Exhausted*

You truly do expend more energy doing less in Asia. Adjusting to jet lag, getting to your business appointments on time, maneuvering through crowds on the street, finding a cab, and haggling with a shopkeeper over prices when you are trying to pick up a few souvenirs can be pretty exhausting.

ATTITUDE ADJUSTMENT

Recognizing that any uncomfortable or negative feelings are normal will help alleviate your discomfort. It's also helpful to know that others have similar reactions. Remind yourself that you are in Asia for a purpose and that you'll be going home when your job is done. Following are some suggestions that may help ease your adjustment.

➤ Take care of yourself. Get plenty of sleep and be careful about what you eat and drink. Get daily exercise.

➤ Relax. When the noise and crowds get to you, take some time out for yourself and relax. Consider bringing a tape deck and a relaxation tape with you to listen to for twenty minutes a day. Relax in a bubble bath.

➤ Don't mope around your hotel room. Stay active. Jog, swim, or join a *tai chi* group. Take a walk through a local park or visit a museum. Re-center yourself by focusing on your strengths and following your interests.

➤ Keep your sense of humor. Look for the amusing aspects of your situation. At least you will have lots of good stories to tell when you get home. Laughter releases tension.

➤ Know you are envied. Many people appreciate the exotica of other cultures and would give their eyeteeth to be in your position. This should bring you some sense of satisfaction.

MORE ADVICE

A Touch of Home
When I travel overseas, I do so for long periods of time. One thing that has helped me to adjust is that I rearrange the furniture in the hotel

room. I know that sounds silly but I set it up in the most comfortable way for my working needs. Some people call it "nesting," I guess. I also bring some things from home like photos of loved ones, my own pillow and shower mat, my Walkman and favorite tapes. (Bel Air, California)

Travel with a Companion

I think it is always best to travel with someone else, if you can. I recall going to Hong Kong on a layover with another colleague. It helped tremendously. You could tell that we were pretty uncomfortable about the new environment, but it was really easy for one of us to convince the other to do something. We stuck together like glue until we felt comfortable. By the end of the weekend, we ventured out on our own a bit. Hong Kong is a pretty tame place to start your Asian experience. I think it is the easiest place in the East to adjust to. Many Westerners call it a "Western oasis in the Far East." I think it's a good place to decompress if you have spent too many days in some of the less-developed countries. (Dublin, Ireland)

STEPS YOU CAN TAKE

This may be your only opportunity to visit Asia. You will miss a lot if you leave for your destination cold, then confine yourself to your hotel and meeting rooms. No matter what your interests, if you take the time to learn about your destination, prepare for your trip, and take a look around when you get there, you are bound to find something that will intrigue or please you.

Before You Go

➤ Read up on the culture you will be visiting. Books, films, videos, and talking to others who have lived in or traveled to your destination are great resources to help prepare you for your visit.

➤ Get to know the people you will visit. Use phone, fax, or letter to initiate your relationships. A friendly reception is more likely to await you when you arrive.

➤ Plan your days. Find activities that will help you fill your spare time.

If you are very busy, you will have little time to experience culture shock.

➤ List places you think you might want to visit. Jotting down interesting day and evening destinations will give you a selection of possible places to visit in your spare time.

➤ Learn a few phrases in the native language. Knowing "please" and "thank you" in the local tongue is appreciated and is the key to opening doors.

➤ Practice using chopsticks. If you think you would be uncomfortable using chopsticks in a formal setting, practice before you go. You may also want to try restaurants featuring the cuisine of the country you plan to visit. You can take in the atmosphere and try to find out which foods you are comfortable with before you go overseas.

When You Get There

EASE IN

➤ Try to travel with someone. If it is your first trip, don't go alone if you can possibly avoid it, or meet up with a local business associate when you arrive.

➤ Stay in a quality Western-style hotel if you can afford to. A poor-quality hotel may result in loss of sleep, which could ruin your trip and your experience, not to mention put a kink in your positive business attitude.

➤ Choose a hotel that offers some extras. A hotel with a pool, health club, restaurants, shops, and planned entertainment becomes a comfortable place to spend some quality time. Even if you don't get out of the hotel this trip, you will at least be able to get out of your room.

➤ Make your hotel room comfortable. Bring something to make it feel homey and arrange it to suit your needs.

➤ Tell your Asian hosts it is your first visit. They may spend more time with you if they know you are there for the first time, and may even make arrangements for you or help you arrange to see some cultural events or take a tour. Most hosts will appreciate your interest in their country and culture, and this will help enhance your relationship.

EXPLORE

➤ Take a city tour soon after you arrive. This is a safe and comfortable way to become familiar with your new environment. Tours in English can usually be booked at the hotel, where you will be picked up and dropped off afterward. Tours also provide a good opportunity to meet other travelers.

➤ Do a little bit of sightseeing each day. Visiting even one city site on the way back to your hotel from a meeting or on the way to lunch or dinner will help give you a deeper understanding of the culture and the people.

➤ Get a walking map and explore. Your hotel will provide a map of the surrounding area at your request. A walk through the neighborhood will help you see how people live and work. Of course we recommend that you walk only during daylight hours and in safe areas.

➤ Hire a driver or use a taxi. Renting a car in Asia may be more than you can or would want to handle. In all Four Tigers, however, public transportation is your best bet—outside commuter hours.

➤ Plan your travel routes. Keep the telephone numbers of taxis and bus and train route maps with you, as well as a card from your hotel in the local language in case you get lost. City maps can easily be obtained from tourist offices at the airport or downtown as well as from your hotel.

➤ Establish familiar grounds. Frequenting certain lunch and dinner spots and evening hangouts will help you establish a rapport with the owners and locals and make you feel like you're more part of the group.

➤ Talk to locals who speak English. They appreciate the chance to practice their English and will be delighted at your interest in their culture and more than happy to answer your questions about it.

ADAPT

➤ Be flexible. Allow plenty of time to get to appointments. Bring a book to read in case you have to wait. Try to figure out ways to avoid offending your hosts while satisfying your own needs.

➤ Be patient. People in Asia are not as direct or usually in as much of a rush as people in the West. When you feel yourself getting uptight, take a few deep breaths and visualize a calming scene. Remember that people won't behave a certain way just because you want them to, and getting upset won't make you or them feel any better.

➤ Ask your Asian hosts questions about their country and culture. They will usually enjoy talking about it, which will help you better understand and appreciate what you are seeing.

➤ Develop friendships by showing interest in your hosts. This, in turn, will help overcome what you may initially perceive as being a negative environment.

➤ Keep an open mind. Look for similarities and intriguing differences between your culture and the one you are visiting. Focus on the good aspects. Try role reversal—how would you react if a foreign business person visiting you in the United States insisted that their way of living and doing business was the only way? When you're in another country, remember to do as the locals do, since it is *your* ways that may seem strange or offensive to them.

➤ Appreciate the countries you visit for their special qualities and lifestyles. Do not compare them to your own country or you may offend your host.

➤ Take a cue from your Asian counterparts. When you feel confused, embarrassed, or upset, smile, smile, smile.

2 | *Doing Business Nine to Five*

When I go to Taiwan, the company slogan is "The customer is always first." When I go to a Korean company, it is "Join us and win," or "Jump on the bandwagon." In Singapore it is "Smile, even when the customer is wrong," and in Hong Kong it's "Let's make a deal." (Cupertino, California)

When doing business in the Four Tigers, it is important to understand the basic differences between these Asian cultures and your own. If you have a good, overall understanding of these differences and approach your Asian business contacts in an open-minded, nonconfrontational spirit, you will have paved the way to successful business dealings.

CONFUCIAN ETHICS

You will find that each of the Four Tigers has its own business personality, but underneath lie common bonds. Hong Kong, Taiwan, and Singapore are primarily Chinese-based cultures, since all three areas were settled by Chinese. Korea has its own distinct culture, though it has been greatly influenced by both China and Japan. All four cultures place great value on Confucian ethics, interpreted over the last nearly 2,500 years to suit the cultural milieu of the times.

The Confucian ethics of loyalty to the state and the sacrifice of personal goals for the benefit of the state have been translated in modern times to loyalty to the company and the sacrifice of personal goals for those of the company. Hierarchy and rank developed from the principle of filial piety, with the result that social rankings range from high to low in the relationships between male and female, elder and younger, state and worker. Confucius taught that hard work brought honor to the state and to the worker and that compassion and righteousness, harmony, consensus, and the use of rituals, etiquette, and ceremony form the foundation for all good relationships.

Some in the Four Tiger countries claim, however, that the Confucian principles of restraint, moderation, and living a simple life have given way to a relatively new interpretation—the duty of everyone to strive to become as rich as possible. Contemporary Confucian scholar Dr. Sinn Whor Shu of Singapore has been quoted as saying that "Confucius strongly advocated making money to the best of one's ability."[1] Dr. Sinn believes this to be a more appropriate principle for today's business world.

This interpretation of Confucian ethics has been used by Asian leaders including Lee Kuan Yew, former president of Singapore; Chun Doo Hwan, former president of Korea; and Chiang Kai-shek, who set up the Nationalist China government. The rationale behind the establishment of their authoritarian leaderships was that it helped steer their nations into becoming profit-oriented economies.

ASIAN SOCIAL CONVENTIONS

While many businesspeople in the Four Tiger countries have had Western educations and years of international experience, many of those born before 1950 retain traditional attitudes and customs. As a Western businessperson, it is very important that you respect and observe Asian cultural and social customs, particularly how they apply to the business world. Doing so will help you build the solid relationships necessary to make headway in your business dealings.

Status

Status, meaning how you are placed in the social and business hierarchy, forms the framework for all interactions. It is still of the utmost importance in all Asian countries to acknowledge and show courtesy to persons of the highest rank first. Introductions, invitations, and seating arrangements are all made according to rank. Age is also honored, so the older members of any group are also the first to be acknowledged.

Modesty

Keqi (*k'o-hsi*) the preeminent Confucian concept of courtesy, humility, and morality, is the foundation of all essential Asian social and business behaviors. Westerners frequently overreact to this Asian politeness, feeling patronized or intimidated. *Keqi* encompasses personal as well as family, business, and financial humility. In contrast, Westerners tend to brag about their accomplishments as well as those of their family, business, and country. Asians consider this arrogant.

Harmony

Above all, it is important to maintain harmony within the group. Your Asian associates will do everything in their power to ensure that meetings go smoothly, including giving you a yes rather than their real answer if they think the truth might upset you.

Saving Face

It is also important to understand the concept of *mian-zi* (*mien-tzu*), or face. Traditional Confucian values are based on human feelings rather than religious values. Accordingly, respect for and sensitivity to the feelings of others and their self-image and status is very important. Asians are very aware of slights to self-image or status and are careful not to slight others.

If an Asian loses face, which is equal to being socially discredited, he or she can no longer function effectively in the community. The reputation of a company or country is similarly affected. Accordingly, Asians will go to considerable lengths to avoid harming the reputations of their coworkers and countrymen. It is therefore important for Westerners to avoid criticism or ridicule, even if it may seem warranted. It usually makes the situation worse, since the criticized party may even seek revenge. While the revenge may be verbal, it can also be more concrete and damaging to you and your enterprise.

Be careful to exercise diplomacy in any situation where criticism, discipline, differences of opinion, or anger is involved. Make your point and save the other person's face. Remember also that Asians tend to smile when they are embarrassed. If someone should accidentally spill tea in your lap, don't get mad. Smile and graciously accept his or her apology.

Intermediaries

The higher one is on the social ladder, the greater the concern with saving face. Many VIPs are so concerned about offending or being offended, which could irreparably damage their social status, that they use intermediaries, or third parties, in both their personal and business dealings. *Mian-zi* is difficult to assess if people are just meeting or don't know each other very well, and people of lesser status may find it difficult to deal with those of higher status. In such situations, an intermediary becomes necessary if business is to be accomplished. There are companies that specialize in negotiating agreements between Western and Eastern firms, earning commissions for the introductions and connections they provide. If you are not a large or well-known firm and have no local offices in Asia, you should consider hiring one of these companies to help you get started. They can make the contacts for you, set the terms, and help you find partners.

Relationships

Friendly associations are very important to Asians, so they will try to become "friends" as quickly as possible to break the ice. You should remember, however, that declarations of friendship refer not to a personal relationship but to the relationship between your two companies. How close relationships become varies from culture to culture. Koreans tend to take longer to initiate friendships but, once developed, they become quite strong. The Chinese are initially friendlier, but it takes some time to develop a firm relationship.

Western businesspeople do business on the basis of product, price, profit, and service. For Asians, it is *guan-xi* (*kuan-hsi*), incorporating personal contact, trust, commitment, and obligation, that is the most important part of the business relationship. In Asia, business dealings begin on a company-to-company basis but are maintained on a personal level. It is very important that your Asian business counterparts like and trust you. They must believe that you are knowledgeable and dedicated and will follow the rules and abide by fair business practices.

Consensus

While the Four Tigers generally do not close big deals immediately, they do tend to make decisions more quickly than the Japanese. New ideas, however, are not received well; they must be thought through and discussed internally. Do not force your counterparts to respond immediately and directly to a presentation. They may need to refer the ideas to their group to reach a consensus in order to avoid any assumption of personal responsibility. It is important that you be well informed about your own company and its goals and as knowledgeable as possible about your Asian counterparts and their goals.

➤ Always be patient and calm. Never speak in absolutes or give ultimatums. Since meetings are seen as interactions between organizations rather than individuals, try to maintain a cooperative stance. Though individuals do not feel responsible for corporate decisions, they will nevertheless lose face in the firm if something goes wrong.

➤ Asian culture runs on teamwork. Each player has a role as an official, an expert, or a supporter. Usually one person facilitates the meeting and allows each player to participate in turn.

ASIAN BUSINESS COURTESIES

Hospitality

In general, you will find that your Asian business contacts are very hospitable. They treat Westerners very well, often providing costly meals or entertainment. Though they appear eager to please, do not interpret their hospitality in Western cultural terms. Rolling out the red carpet does not necessarily mean that you have a close relationship. Most often, the higher rated you are, the greater the hospitality.

Transportation and Accommodations

Asian hosts will often pick up their guests at the airport, reserve hotel accommodations for them, and send someone to pick them up for meetings. Hierarchical ranking takes precedence—the higher the visitor's status, the better the transportation and accommodations. Likewise, when Asian guests visit you in the United States, always be sure that they have transportation from and to the airport and confirmed hotel reservations.

Breaking the Ice

Casual conversation is common and encouraged before business is discussed. You may be asked questions about Western trade policy, since this is an area of great interest to Asian people, who tend to be very well informed. Try to catch up on current affairs with a few hours of selective reading, listening to the radio, and watching television. If you have an opinion, temper it. Avoid debate; give insight on the subject being discussed and then ask your colleagues for their thoughts. With practice you can deftly turn a question around to gain more insight and knowledge about your Asian associates.

GIFTS

While Westerners say thank you and write thank-you notes to express gratitude, Asians prefer to show appreciation in some tangible way, such as through gifts and favors. Initial meetings generally do not require gifts, but gift-giving is a very important part of creating and nurturing relationships with your Asian business associates. Gift-giving is most visible in countries such as Korea and Japan, although many businesspeople in Chinese countries, including Taiwan and Hong Kong, exchange some sort of token gifts. Presents are less likely to be exchanged in Singapore. If you are planning to bring gifts with you to present at a meeting, it is important that you understand basic gift-giving protocol.

Gift Etiquette

> ➤ If you are visiting for the first time and are not sure if gifts are appro-

priate, bring them and exchange them if the gesture is initiated. Gifts should be business related rather than personal items. Conspicuous luxury items could suggest impropriety, particularly in Singapore.

➣ One potential dilemma is that when you present a gift, it may be politely declined. Asian etiquette requires that a gift, favor, or invitation be modestly declined two or three times. You are expected to persist with your offer until the recipient finally accepts. After three tries, however, if you still feel you are receiving a firm refusal, quietly put the gift aside.

➣ In a business setting, your gift will be received with both hands, then most likely put away to be opened later. Asians do not generally open or comment on gifts in public. You may later receive a verbal or written thank you. If your gift is for a company, present it with both hands to the leader of the Asian side, or to each person individually, along with a short speech.

➣ When you receive a gift, accept it graciously with two hands. Thank the gift giver and then put it away with care to be opened later.

➣ Gifts should be wrapped. The manner in which they are wrapped is important. Wrapping paper is fine; however, preferred colors differ country-by-country, and decorative bows are usually not used. A well-wrapped gift shows sincerity and thoughtfulness, while a sloppy wrapping job detracts from the sincerity of the gift.

Gift Suggestions

It can be difficult to select an appropriate gift while you are in Asia. It is best to bring something from your local area that cannot easily be purchased abroad. Gifts with your company logo are usually very well liked. If you are visiting a company and are unsure as to how many gifts to bring, purchase items that can be shared by the office, such as boxes of candy or dried fruits. (See also the individual country chapters.)

Some recommended gifts are:

➣ Items with your company logo such as appointment books, paperweights, pen sets, and key rings. Golf balls are especially appreciated, while women like silk scarves or other decorative accessories.

➣ Western art posters and calendars.

➤ Travel or coffee-table picture books on your home area.

➤ Magazine subscriptions, especially pictorial U.S. magazines or magazines specializing in your Asian associate's field.

➤ Americana, such as pewter collectibles, copies of Colonial wooden toys, bronze ornaments, etc.

➤ Items emblazoned with U.S.A. sports insignias.

➤ For large groups, T-shirts with the company logo or an appropriate slogan/design.

➤ Inscribed crystal bowls or vases.

➤ Liquor, particularly prestigious brands of wines or whiskeys from your local area.

➤ Gourmet foods from your local area.

➤ Boxes of candy, sweets, and fruits that can be shared by the office.

Gifts to Avoid

Generally, avoid consumer electronics, clothes, and anything that can be easily purchased locally. Women may also want to avoid giving flowers, personal items, or gifts for the family, unless you know them very well. Also avoid oversized gifts or breakables since your Asian contacts may be traveling, and these would be, at any rate, a burden for you to carry.

Each country has particular items that should not be given as gifts. These are explained in the individual country chapters.

GENERAL BUSINESS ETIQUETTE

➤ Do not cold call in Asia. Personal contacts and relationships are important and must be established first. If you are establishing business for the first time overseas use a third-party agent to help set up your initial meetings. You can secure one through your local consulate or business organizations. Women in particular should use an agent since it is doubly hard for a woman to establish herself in Asia.

➤ Have your business card translated on the reverse side into the language of the country you are visiting. This adds to your credibility since it is perceived as a company investment in you, and it also indicates that you have an interest in the culture. Korea uses Korean *hangul* phonetic characters. Taiwan uses Mandarin Chinese characters. English is acceptable in Singapore and Hong Kong, although Chinese is a nice touch. Most Chinese in Hong Kong still speak Cantonese, although Mandarin is gaining in popularity due to Hong Kong's planned reversion to China in 1997. Most Singaporean Chinese speak Mandarin.

➤ Initiate a handshake if one has not been offered to you. Your Asian counterparts may not initiate a handshake with a woman since this is not customary in their culture.

➤ Pay attention to the seating protocol in Asian cultures. Meeting participants are seated according to rank or function (host, guest of honor, primary speakers, administrative personnel). If you are a woman in a key position, consult with your colleagues to be sure you are placed in a seat commensurate with your position.

➤ Remain standing until the host invites you to sit down, unlike in Western cultures, where the men stand and women sit.

➤ Make it a point to learn some phrases in the language of the country you are visiting. For Korea, learn some Korean phrases. For Singapore and Taiwan, learn some Mandarin, and for Hong Kong, Cantonese. (See the simple phrases at the end of each country chapter.)

➤ Do your homework. Not all Asian countries are the same. Read up on the countries you are visiting and understand the differences in their culture and business protocol as well as their historical and economic backgrounds.

➤ Service your accounts. If you are in sales, keep up with your clients after the deals are made. Continuous follow-through is expected.

➤ Unlike the Western preference for long, complicated contracts, the Koreans and Chinese prefer short documents, since they believe that business results from the relationship between two firms rather than from the documents both have signed. Shorter documents are also easier to translate.

Correspondence

Each of the Four Tigers uses distinctive salutations and closings for letters and faxes. Generally, however, your correspondence can begin with, "To my respected (title) (full name)." In Chinese cultures and in Korea (as in Japan), the family name usually appears first in native usage. However, some Asian businesspeople will give their personal names first in their overseas correspondence or will adopt Western names (like "James") to make it easier for you to remember their names. Sometimes it is difficult to figure out which is the family name. In written correspondence you should, therefore, use the full name as you've received it from the addressee. When meeting someone in Asia it is perfectly acceptable to ask that person how he or she would like to be addressed.

The closing paragraph of your letter should include a statement of good wishes and business cooperation and success. If you expect a reply, mention this in your letter.

Keep your English simple and list your points in easy-to-read bullet items.

Phone Etiquette

➤ If you are phoning your Asian counterpart, state your name, title, and company and then ask for the individual you are trying to reach.

➤ Learn enough of the language to be able to ask for the person you want to speak to.

➤ Keep phone conversations courteous but short and to the point.

➤ As with person-to-person communications, give the person on the other end of the line your undivided attention. Do not hold an outside conversation, eat, or do other things while you are on the phone. This is usually obvious to the other party, who may view it as a lack of interest or respect.

➤ If you must look up information or find a report, tell your party that you will call back rather than have someone wait while you go through your files.

➤ If you are holding a telephone meeting, have the agenda in front of you to keep your phone call on track.

➤ Make your own phone calls. It is best to contact the person directly instead of through an intermediary. You will come across as more personal and sincere.

➤ Call for a reason. Your Asian contacts are busy; keep to the point so they won't feel you are keeping them from their work.

➤ When you end the call, be sure to repeat and summarize the points made during the conversation to be sure both sides understand each other's position. Also, thank the person for his or her time and make a positive statement, such as saying how informative the call was.

➤ If you are disconnected, call back immediately. Disconnections are frequent during intra-Asian as well as U.S.–Asia calls.

➤ If you are using an answering machine instead of company voice-mail, make sure your greeting is professional and without music or other background noise.

BUSINESS MEETING BASICS

Connections

Establish a network of personal connections on both official and personal levels. Carefully cultivate them through regular contact. Consistency can reap big rewards, since the system is set up to serve the most familiar and thus most trusted customer first. Women can and should develop many-leveled relationships with their Asian contacts. Some women we interviewed said that they also try to develop relationships with their associates' families, and that these can be a valuable asset in their business dealings.

Some Westerners complain that their Asian business associates seem to be changing prices, quality, and other commitments from one day to the next. This puts a big strain on the relationship. But it should not happen to you if you take the time to build a proper relationship by developing open communication channels and by proving yourself to be trustworthy. Asian businesspeople attach great importance to their relationships with family members, classmates, and people from the same town, often giving them special consideration. Who you know in addition to what you know is accordingly very important.

Punctuality

Be on time for business meetings. In Asia, punctuality is often considered a reflection of your interest and sincerity.

Introductions

When conducting business in Asia, arrive with written introductions from one or more people who are known and respected by your Asian counterparts. This is important for newcomers, particularly women, since it is the best way to clearly state your credentials. If an introduction cannot be made in person, it can be handled by phone or fax. When you are introduced, state your credentials again during your first meeting. Women should not overlook this valuable method of building credibility. Overemphasizing your credentials, however, is considered impolite. To ensure you have given them adequate exposure, have a colleague highlight your achievements, when appropriate.

The handshake is now a common form of greeting, although some bowing may be evident among older Asians. Women should initiate a handshake if one is not offered. Many times Asians do not know how to approach a businesswoman and will not think to extend their hand in a greeting.

Business Cards

Business cards are a necessity. They should be presented during introductions and at the beginning of meetings. Your card should clearly identify your company, title, and name. Be sure that your title is one that can be easily understood, such as manager, director, or senior buyer. Titles such as "specialist" or "consultant" will not clearly convey your position within your firm.

> ➤ It is a good idea to have cards translated into the local language of the company you are visiting. Your business associates will be impressed and pleased with this gesture, which will also enhance your credibility; it shows that your firm has invested in you and expects you to be an

active participant in the meetings and business at hand. Have your business cards printed with your name and title in English on one side and translated into the local language on the reverse.

> If you are not able to get your card translated and printed before you leave, there are business-card translation firms in the countries you will visit. Many hotels can help you with your cards. The most common way to format your cards in Asia is to have your name and title printed in the local characters vertically from top to bottom, right to left on the back of the card. Make sure your printer is knowledgeable about card conventions and formats. Always have a proofreader advise you on the best way to have your name transliterated into the target language, and always check the spelling and pronunciation of every detail before printing. Be sure you order enough cards so you won't run out; businesspeople can hand out as many as fifty cards during a large business session.

> Use both hands to present your business card so that your name can be easily read by the recipient. Accept your counterparts' business cards with both hands. Look at each card carefully and read it. Hold on to it instead of shoving it into a pocket or purse. Place the card in front of you at the meeting table for easy reference. Do not let the person who gave you the card see you make any notations on it. This is seen as defacing the card and is considered disrespectful.

The Agenda

Asian hosts organize meetings from start to finish, from introductions to seating order, meeting format, and content. They try to ensure that the meeting will go smoothly and that there will be no surprises. Therefore, you should prepare and present your agenda to your Asian associates in advance. They should be briefed about the subjects to be discussed and the sequence that will be followed and asked if they have any additions or changes they would like to make to the proposed meeting format. If this is not done, lengthy delays may develop during the meeting while your counterparts discuss each agenda item internally and seek to enlist the appropriate people to join the discussion.

Translators

If you decide that you need a translator, be sure you get one who is familiar with the technical terms used in your industry. Try to get someone who has been recommended by other Western firms rather than one recommended by the company with whom you are planning to do business. Spend some time with the interpreter reviewing your expectations, the proposed agenda, the possible negotiations, and the technical presentation material. Avoid using jargon or slang since your translator is not likely to be familiar with it.

Presentations

Handouts and visual aids will enhance your presentation and make it easier for observers to understand. Charts outlining each major point are well received. Presentations should be brief. Offer solid facts with documented sources in a friendly, low-key but persuasive manner. Use natural, clearly enunciated English throughout and allow time for questions. (For more suggestions, see Appendix 1, "Presentations.")

Seating

Hierarchical relationships are acknowledged through seating placement. While the high-ranking Western executive is usually preceded into the room by his staff, the reverse is true in Asia. The head executive enters first, sometimes followed by an interpreter. As a general rule, the speakers for each group sit at the center of the conference table facing each other with their staffs seated around them in descending rank and order of importance.

Chinese-style meetings, as conducted in Hong Kong, Taiwan, and Singapore, have more informal seating arrangements. A round conference table may be used. The highest-ranking person will usually conduct the meeting and act as the spokesperson.

In Korea, business meetings, much like in Japan, are conducted around rectangular tables, with the highest-ranking participant sitting in the center with his key contributor on his right. The lowest-ranking participant will sit closest to the door to attend to errands. The guests sit together on the side of the table near the wall that is furthest from the door. This is called the "wall of honor." The highest-ranking member or

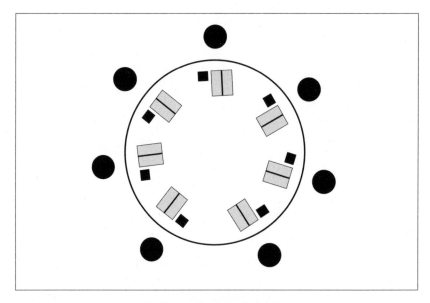

Chinese Business Seating

the speaker will take the seat in the center of the table opposite the host, facing the door. The ends of the table are usually left vacant.

If you are confused about the seating arrangements, take your cue from your hosts and where they are seated to locate your seat. If you are host to the meeting, ask your Asian colleagues in advance to provide you with a list of their attendees and the rank of each. While some recommend using place cards, it is usually easier for you as host to indicate where your guests are to be seated.

Set-up

Water glasses, tablets, and writing instruments, plus any charts, transparencies for overhead projectors (OHPs), or leave-behinds are generally on the table at each seat before the meeting begins.

Speakers

The highest-ranking Chinese in the group acts as spokesperson for the whole group. The Korean spokesperson, however, may not be the highest-ranking. The top person may, nevertheless, readily join the discussion.

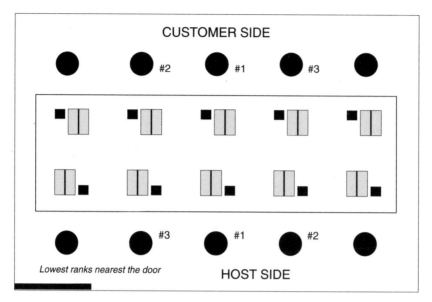

Korean Business Seating

Breaks

If you are holding a meeting, arrange for at least one break during the morning and afternoon sessions to allow your guests to refresh themselves.

Have cold drinks, coffee, tea, and light snacks available. Also provide a separate room for your counterparts in case they need to discuss something among themselves.

Meals

Meals are an important part of doing business in Asia. Allow time for meals with your Asian counterparts, whether you are a guest or host. The business dinner, in particular, is a critical extension of the business meeting. Businesspeople are expected to accept dinner invitations when on business in Asia and to host dinners when they are receiving Asian guests.

Women should be sure to attend business dinners and consider them to be part of the business day. Do not bow out. (See Chapter 5, "Dining.")

Negotiations East and West

When you enter into business negotiations with your Asian counter-parts, it is important that you understand how they view the negotia-tions from their own cultural perspective. A successful Western businesswoman not only needs to understand how her Asian associate conducts business, but also how she can keep up with her associate so that the meetings proceed smoothly and stick to the agenda, with each point understood clearly by both sides.

Western-style Business

Westerners tend to debate, question, and challenge points presented at business meetings. We are quick to jump into a presentation or business discussion and stay with it long into dinner and afterward. We tend to be direct and to focus our efforts on completing the task at hand. We use a competitive and confrontational communications style. Westerners usu-ally operate under some kind of time pressure, which sometimes leads to us betraying our impatience during protracted business meetings. In gen-eral, we approach a meeting with target deadlines for signatures and clo-sure. One individual with the approval of upper management can have full control of the decision-making process.

When Westerners make an agreement, it is usually the value of the deal that makes it attractive. Westerners are not as concerned about whom they buy their products and services from since they are more concerned with cost, features, and value for the money. We tend to approach a product or sale from a marketing standpoint, trying to weigh the value and opportunities the products offer our customers. When cre-ating product packages, Westerners will keep trying to improve the deal with features or enhancements before making their final offer. Western-ers believe in contracts and adhere to their terms.

Asian-style Business

Asians use the business meeting for information gathering, for present-ing ideas, and for developing consensus. Much of the material they want to cover at the meeting can therefore seem either obvious or even intru-sive to the Westerner. While the idea of privacy is growing in Asia, it still does not meet Western expectations. You may be asked what Westerners consider to be very personal questions, such as your age or your salary. Some businesspersons have also expressed concern about business privacy. Most Asian firms know everything about their competitors' activities within the region. Accordingly, they may ask you questions about competitors that you may not wish to answer. Try to deal with these issues tactfully without causing a loss of face. These questions are actually efforts by your Asian associates to get to know you and their competition better. It is important for Asians to trust the people they work with even before the quality and reliability of the products are taken into consideration.

The Four Tigers can seem very blunt and direct in their dealings with Westerners. The Koreans can also be emotional. They have the strongest, most visible pride of the four groups. A discussion with Koreans can take a turn for the worse if they feel you have issued them a challenge. The Chinese tend be more forthright, so their business dealings may appear more aggressive than those of the Koreans.

These four Asian cultures do not resolve issues or make decisions at the negotiating table. This is done in between or after meetings. It is customary for them to informally and unofficially drop hints and make inquiries outside of the meeting rooms during breaks and in the evening. When things are not going well, they may deliberately delay proceedings through a variety of tactics rather than admit that something is not working out. Or your associates may report that things are going well when they are not. You must therefore exercise caution before accepting anything at face value. Keep your antennae up and your feelers out.

The Four Tigers do not look upon a contract as being the end of the negotiations. To them it is just the beginning of a relationship that will change continuously as it is reevaluated and renegotiated.

Evaluating Your Progress

Western business negotiations generally have two stages: the business close followed by smooth implementation of the agreement. For the four Asian Tigers, there are three stages: the social relationship, the talks leading to the signing of the agreement, and the give-and-take of the working relationship after the contract has been signed. This is where problems generally arise. In their desire to ensure harmony, Asians may give answers they believe Westerners want to hear rather than true answers.

This can prevent you from obtaining a realistic picture of what is going on and lead you to assume that the deal has come to closure. Complications arise when you proceed as if the deal has been closed and the Asians continue to explore more areas for compromise. A savvy businesswoman will therefore continue to assess whether every aspect of the business discussion has been accepted to ensure that both sides are comfortable with each point of the agreement before moving on to the next.

Participants

Westerners and Chinese usually send only one or two people to business meetings to be responsible for the negotiations and decisions. Westerners expect that this limited staff can cover all the issues. Often these participants are prepared to present terms and conditions to close a deal with their Asian counterparts. The Koreans, much like the Japanese, generally bring more people who are adept in their field of expertise so that all the information is directly at hand. It is very difficult for Koreans to understand how one person could be knowledgeable enough to represent all the corporate disciplines and answer all the possible questions that could arise. Westerners likewise may wonder how Asians can afford to send so many staff members and allow them to take off so much time. If you cannot bring your team along, offer to carry back questions you can't answer or locate the needed information by faxing or phoning the head office.

> ➤ When planning a meeting on your home ground, it is helpful to know who is planning to attend the meeting and to match the attendees one on one with your own staff members.

Modifying Your Style

When you are negotiating with your Asian counterparts you should adjust your style to something more compatible with the culture in which you are working. For most Westerners, this usually means toning things down. For example, Asian companies are often hierarchical, but every level has input in the final decision. In contrast, we Westerners tend to focus on the key decision-maker, such as the president, to ultimately endorse our products or presentations; since we have less regard for hierarchy than our Asian counterparts we will often try to jump ranks. Using this Western style in Asia is not advisable. Rather, you should operate within the Asian system and gradually elevate your ideas from lower to upper management.

Westerners talk more than listen. We use business meetings to brainstorm, throwing out ideas and examining them on the spot. Asians, on the other hand, use business meetings to share information on issues that have already been resolved. Working with Asia can accordingly be frustrating if you work on short deadlines—or rewarding if you have patience and endurance. Have the patience to listen to your Asian counterparts and watch their body language as they speak. Often a yes is used simply to acknowledge your statement. Westerners often misinterpret this as solid agreement and easily become distraught later when they find they have not closed the deal.

Work with your Asian counterparts, not against them. Focus your negotiations on how they will benefit both of you. And, finally, know both your products and theirs. Knowing your product line and understanding how it can fit into their strategy will help strengthen your position. View the negotiations as a key to establishing and retaining a long-term relationship. Take care to work out any points of disagreement that may arise during your discussions.

WORKING WITH YOUR TEAM

Traveling with a team is the ideal way to conduct business in Asia. The team approach relieves any one individual of responsibility for the outcome of the trip and adds to your company's credibility. Understandably, sending a team is not often possible, so arranging for a conference call or phoning or faxing individuals for updates in between meetings can be a way to include missing team members.

Westerners have generally been more successful in Asia when they have adopted a team approach. Companies that have worked with Japan have learned to focus on group thinking and quality circles. Though the Chinese are willing to handle business on a more individual basis, the Koreans prefer to work in teams. For businesswomen, who can easily be ignored in male-dominated groups, understanding team tactics is especially important.

Before Your Trip

If you decide to take a team, a pre-meeting is essential. Meet with your colleagues before you leave on your trip, if possible, and definitely before you meet your Asian associates, to discuss each person's role and the agenda and to map out a strategy you can all agree on. Problems can occur when you have not worked out your strategy beforehand.

During the pre-meeting, make sure you clarify the team members' individual roles and responsibilities. If a team member has a problem accepting your direction, a solution should be worked out in advance. A stronger, more cohesive team will develop when each person plays his or her part and defers, when appropriate, to other team members. If your team has a mix of men and women, review tactics on how to work together to establish the credibility and authority of each teammate.

The team needs to reinforce the credibility of its female participants. While the easiest solution would seem to be to have a male in the lead position, it is not the best in the long run. Instead, advise your male colleagues that they need to use their influence to reinforce the positions of the female team members during the meeting.

Women also need to prep their male colleagues on more particular situations that can arise and how to handle them. For example, your Asian counterparts may see the oldest male team member in your group as the senior member. The best way to handle this is for all team members to defer to the highest-ranking member at the meeting.

On Arrival

The organizer of the trip can help set the tone for the team by reviewing the agenda, emphasizing the meeting protocol and reminding team members of the Asian expectations for dress, stressing conservative attire. He or she can set up the social agenda (dinner is enough, after-hours drinking is not necessary) or even suggest after-dinner alternatives. Team leaders can also suggest that the group stay in the same hotel for team support, discussion, and sessions.

➤ Teams should plan to stick together. If you can't stay at the same hotel, at least organize pre- and post-meetings for each session or meet together as often as you can.

➤ A pre-meeting should be held to decide which role each member is to play and to choose a person to coordinate the meeting agenda as well as a facilitator to organize materials and help members focus on their roles. Clarify all points of internal concern before the meeting, including who is to respond to which points, take notes, speak for which field, and coordinate the meeting as well as who will take on the administrative role, should the need arise. This will help avoid such male "slips" as asking you to make copies.

➤ Post-meeting conclaves allow you to review the presentations and negotiations, explore any pertinent issues among the group, brainstorm new ideas, and plan any changes in strategy.

➤ Take the time to clarify the needs of your Asian associates.

➤ When team participants are of equal rank, it is even more important for each participant to stick to his or her area of expertise. If there is no hierarchy, at least each person can be associated with a particular specialty.

➤ If you are bilingual, make sure you will not be used as a translator during meetings and discussions.

➤ It is very important that team members not bicker, interrupt each other, or talk at the same time during a meeting. If a woman is running the meeting, this rule is even more important since discord will reflect poorly on her leadership capabilities.

AT THE MEETING

Preparations

➤ Asians prefer to use an agenda, with designated team roles, hierarchy at the table, and a time and place for each person to speak. Decisions have usually been determined before the meeting and any changes are discussed off line. Western meeting style, including the use of free association, exploratory communication, and brainstorming, appears disorganized to most Asian cultures. If you have ideas, share them in your own private sessions, either after the meeting or before the next meeting.

> Business agendas should include a list of participants and their titles. If you are supplying the agenda for a meeting you will be attending, make sure to include your name and title. This will advertise in writing that you will be an active participant at the business meeting.

> In the agenda, list the titles of your team with those of highest rank at the top. Make sure your rank and title are aligned with that of your Asian counterpart.

> If you are planning a trip to Asia or are having clients visit you, make sure you give plenty of advance notice so they can make travel plans and prepare an agenda. Asian travel routes are very busy, especially around the holidays; as long as three weeks may be required to book a flight.

> Set an agenda in advance so that each side has an opportunity to enhance or change it and make all necessary preparations for the meeting.

> Secure an appropriate meeting room before your guests arrive. Make sure it is large enough and has enough chairs, proper lighting, and audio/video equipment.

> Present your ideas in advance of a meeting either by fax message or in writing. Invite your Asian counterparts to add their input as you are preparing your proposal. If you actively involve your counterparts, they will be better able to participate when you are meeting face to face.

Introductions

> When you are introducing Asian participants to your executives, introduce the Asian participant first.

> When you are introducing an Asian visitor to your firm, introduce his or her name, title, and company, in that order.

> When you are introducing visiting Asian senior and junior executives, introduce the senior executives first, from the most senior on down.

> When you are meeting someone again who appears not to remember

you, state your name and title first to avoid any embarrassment on their part.

> When you are saying good-bye, escort your guests back to the main exit, shake their hands, and express your appreciation for their visit.

Participation

> Be punctual. Being late for your business meetings indicates a lack of respect.

> If you are holding the meeting, make both the opening remarks and concluding thoughts. Invite your guests to be seated at the beginning and stand to show your guests out the door when the meeting is over.

> If you are attending a meeting overseas, allow your Asian host to begin and end the meeting.

> Be attentive. Many Westerners tend to multitask during meetings, looking at their notes, letters, and so forth as they listen. Asians take this as a lack of interest.

> Do not push for a decision on the spot. Many times your Asian associates will have already made a decision but will need to discuss the points with their headquarters before finalizing it. Pushing will cause them to lose face.

> Listen actively. You will be more effective if you listen and question the Asian participants rather than simply respond to them.

> Do not finish someone else's sentences or cut off anyone who is speaking, even if they are struggling with the language. Be patient and allow each person the chance to complete their statement.

> Questions may be asked that no team member can answer. Too often an individual may try to "wing it," which reflects very poorly on the team. A better way to handle this is to say, "I do not know the answer to this but will get back to you on it."

> Silences and abrupt interruptions of conversations are common in Asia. Often they allow the team to think through a point or discuss it among themselves. Teams are much more effective when they learn to allow periods of silence instead of jumping in to say something just to fill up the vacuum.

> As moderator, if you sense a misunderstanding, try to elicit the viewpoints of both parties by asking questions until you feel that both parties understand the points that have been made. Women are often thought of as being more adept at sensing and mediating misunderstandings by Asians, and this can give them an advantage.

Language and Temperament

It is common for the Chinese to speak in exaggerated, flowery terms. It is also characteristic of them to be vague and ambiguous to avoid losing face, either their own or someone else's. Irene Parks, an American cross-cultural communications expert, says that 80 percent of the Chinese language is an attempt to avoid accepting responsibility or making commitments. The Western businessperson should therefore be alert to certain key expressions such as "it is inconvenient," which translates to "forget it." They also use "maybe" or "perhaps," which can both be interpreted as either "yes" or "maybe after further discussion."

> Do not mistake Asian deference and hospitality as demonstrations of trust in you. You are an outsider until you have won their trust. Koreans may appear to be somewhat aggressive until they trust you. In the Chinese cultures, lack of trust may result in overpoliteness and the withholding of information.

> Tone down your voice, since a loud voice can be interpreted as being aggressive or angry. Avoid any display of emotion, which is viewed as a loss of self-control. Asian men consider the expression of emotion a negative female trait.

> Frame open-ended questions that can be answered in sentences rather than yes-no questions. Sentence-type answers will help indicate whether or not your point has been understood. Your counterparts will often smile and agree even when they don't understand in an effort to maintain harmony at the meeting.

> Restrain your typically Western tendency to use broad facial expressions and gestures, as they can be unsettling to your counterparts. Your listeners will end up watching your arms moving about and hear little of what you have to say.

> Be decisive and to the point, since women are thought to be easily flustered, sentimental, and indecisive.

➤ Western-style frankness is not appreciated. Be subtle when you speak and become attuned and responsive to the nuances of what your Asian counterparts say.

➤ Since preserving face is critical in Asia, praise is acceptable at the meeting table but any criticisms should be dealt with tactfully.

➤ If you are upset by a remark, somebody's behavior, or an inappropriate suggestion, ignore the remark or politely decline to participate in any activity you find offensive.

Lunch

Asian executives may be too busy to join you for a meal and may ask other office personnel to take you to lunch. In an effort to accommodate you, your hosts may match you with women from their office, thinking you will be more comfortable socializing with them. You should politely decline a lunch with those you view as being lower in rank. Offer instead to take out the senior executives, or tactfully say you have made other plans.

➤ If the Asian executives are above you in rank, they may not feel it would be appropriate for them to take you to lunch. Instead, they may simply choose to visit with you for a short time.

➤ If you host a meeting, announce but do not serve the refreshments yourself. Suggest that everyone help themselves Western style or, if you must serve, ask a male colleague to help you.

➤ Office women in Asia do not need your help when they serve tea; they are salaried employees and take their jobs seriously.

ESTABLISHING YOUR CREDIBILITY

For men, credibility is often derived from their status in the company. For women, credibility is more often derived from their individual skills. A woman therefore has to work doubly hard to establish her credibility. Here are some pointers that will help:

➤ Be visible. Attend and host meetings between your company and your Asian counterparts whenever possible. Travel in Asia is often reserved for decision-makers in a firm, so being present adds to your credibility.

➤ Introductions are important, particularly for women. If you are doing business with a firm for the first time, have yourself introduced by a higher-ranking person in your company who already knows the people you will be dealing with.

➤ If you cannot have someone introduce you, ask a higher-ranking person in your company to send a fax message or correspondence in advance, outlining your title, responsibilities, and background.

➤ Make sure your business card indicates a distinctive title such as "manager" so that your position can be clearly understood. If there is any doubt about your title, it may be automatically assumed that you have a lesser role than others on your team.

➤ To introduce your educational background or other accomplishments, ask your Asian counterparts a leading question such as where they went to school. This will usually prompt them to, in return, inquire about your educational background

➤ Some women wear a school ring or other school jewelry such as a Phi Beta Kappa key or graduate school pendant to subtly advertise their background. Others wear corporate pins designating tenure, thus demonstrating their level of experience.

➤ Asians will often look and respond more to the men on your team than the women. Prepare for this by advising your colleagues of tactics that will help you and the other female members, including making seating arrangements that will place you in a position of authority.

➤ If someone appears confused about your name and rank, offer him another business card, even if you have already given him one. This is a subtle way of reinforcing your title and ensuring acknowledgment of your participation as an active member at the meeting

➤ Women should lead discussions whenever possible. If there is one woman and everyone is of equal rank, let the woman take the lead to help establish her credibility.

➤ A female team leader may experience a problem establishing her credibility unless team members defer to her as the authority figure on the team. Western men need to be aware that their tendency to jump in and answer questions, especially when a woman is speaking, undermines her authority and the team's effectiveness. Women should advise team members not to answer questions directed to her and to otherwise defer to her whenever appropriate. A good response when asked a question that should be directed to a female colleague is, "Jane is the best person to answer that question."

➤ First impressions are lasting. Present yourself in a sincere, confident, professional manner, both in appearance and speech, to create a good first impression. Be yourself. Do not come on overly strong, but don't defer when it is appropriate for you to respond. Deferring to age and position is, however, always acceptable for both sexes.

➤ If the meeting is not going well or if your team is behaving to your disadvantage, call for a break. It is perfectly acceptable in Asia to leave the room for a private discussion or to politely ask your hosts for some time alone. .

➤ Women under thirty-five years of age should try to project a more mature image and avoid discussions of age. Women over thirty-five may want to let their age be known, since age is well respected in Asia.

➤ Avoid being the note taker at the meeting so you won't be viewed as a secretary. If your role includes taking notes, however, just be sure you continue to participate in the give and take as you jot things down.

The Role of the Manager

Managers can be very effective in Asia by helping to enhance their team's credibility. The manager can introduce the staff members by title and outline their areas of expertise, act as moderator to refer questions to the appropriate team member, and highlight the staff's achievements.

➤ It is important that all team members, including management, understand their roles at the meeting and not act out of role. If one of your colleagues is acting out of role, use a break to explain how the group loses face when it is not cohesive.

➤ As a woman, you should advise management that your personal credibility may be jeopardized if your role is undermined, and that this could hinder the success of any follow-up meetings.

➤ Managers can help enhance the credibility of female teammates by reinforcing their authority during the meeting. For example, if a woman is not receiving the appropriate respect, the manager may once again bring attention to her role and authority.

FOR WOMEN ONLY

Basic Business Attire

Business dress is serious business in Asia, where conservative attire is the norm. Asia is also very label conscious. Your success within your firm and field may be assessed by the appropriateness and quality of your outfit. You won't go wrong if you follow the guidelines listed here. (See also individual country chapters for more details.)

➤ Dress conservatively in dark suits. Skirt suits are still considered to be more appropriate, though more pants suits are being seen. Dresses are generally not worn unless covered by a jacket. Stay with blouses rather than sweaters.

➤ Wear muted colors in jewelry and makeup. Avoid bright eye shadows, dangling earrings, and bangle bracelets.

➤ Wear hosiery. Subtle natural shades that complement your outfit are good; avoid tights and fashion colors and designs.

➤ Carry an attaché case, since this conveys a businesslike impression.

➤ Wear low-heeled, dark business shoes. Do not wear red shoes to complement the red pattern in a blouse.

➤ Countries vary in temperature and seasonally can range from extremely cold to suffocatingly hot. It is not appropriate for women to wear low-cut blouses, sleeveless shirts, or go stockingless, even in the warmest climates. Pack linens and cotton suits or a dress and jacket (short-sleeved jackets are popular in business environments). Washable silk items are particularly handy. Find out the average temperature and rain/snowfall before you plan your travel wardrobe.

Hotel Services

Hotels are good places to pick up forgotten toiletries and personal items since their staffs usually speak English. Although hotel prices are usually higher than at home, the hotels generally have the items you'll be needing. Local stores may not carry what you're used to and may also require time and gesturing to communicate your needs.

➤ Hotel laundry and dry-cleaning services are generally very efficient.

➤ Most hotels offer massages and other personal services that are quite good.

➤ Most hotels disapprove of shorts or uncovered shoulders in the lobbies and restaurants.

➤ Bring a one-piece bathing suit if you're planning to use the hotel facilities for a swim. A bathing cap is usually required, as well as pool slippers. They are often provided.

➤ Wear a robe and slippers when walking from your room to the spa or pool.

Toilets/Personal Amenities

Hotels and the better restaurants usually have both Western and Asian toilets. Once you are out in the suburbs, however, you may find only Asian-style toilets. These are basically a ceramic fitting in the floor over which you must squat. Think about maneuvering this one in a skirt and hosiery! Using the Asian toilet takes practice. One woman we know carries a portable female urinal with her to make it easier.

➤ Carry pocket tissue packages with you to dry your hands; they are not usually offered in Asian rest rooms. Handiwipes are good to carry too. In company rest rooms you may see personal towels hanging around the sink. These are owned and used exclusively by individual employees.

➤ Bring personal sanitary items, since you may not find the kind you need or will be unable to ask for them in the local language, especially in outlying districts.

Health

Although immunizations are not usually necessary for the major Asian cities, it is important to check in advance to see if any are required for your particular destination. You can find out by calling your local city or country Department of Health. There is an International Traveler's Hot Line at the Centers for Disease Control and Prevention at (404) 332-4559, or you can write to the Travelers' Health Section at the Centers for Disease Control and Prevention, Atlanta, Georgia 30333. Make sure you let them know about all the countries you plan to visit, including stopovers.

➤ Check with your company to see what medical coverage you have for overseas travel. Some companies may have an overseas medical hot line, while others may have specific hospitals with which they network.

➤ Bring any prescribed medication for allergies, urinary tract infections, diarrhea, respiratory and skin infections, and so forth in clearly labeled prescription bottles.

➤ If you become ill while overseas, ask your hotel to recommend a doctor who speaks English. If you are alone with a male doctor, insist that a female nurse be present during any check-up.

Dealing with Crowds

Asia is crowded, and transportation, especially during rush hours and holidays, can be horrendously trying. Because you may be pressed from all sides, keep your possessions secure and watch for groping male hands. Create a mental shell around yourself and look straight ahead. Avoid catching the eyes of any male passengers around you. (See the individual country chapters for more transportation notes.)

➤ Consider taking a taxi to work to avoid the jam-packed trains, or arrange your schedule so that you won't have to travel during the heaviest commuter hours.

For Asian Businesswomen

Businesswomen of Asian heritage are viewed by Asian men as having less authority than their non-Asian counterparts. Most Asian women we interviewed say that when they are conducting business in Asia they have to be more assertive than they usually are in order to establish their authority and command respect.

Asian businesswomen often bring translators and assistants along with them to help ensure that their managerial position is clearly understood. They suggest that a bilingual businesswoman speak only English to avoid being used as a translator. Otherwise, she should use her language skills strategically to break the ice, to assist when there is a conflict, or during social conversation.

If you are Asian but from a culture different from the one you are visiting, be sure to draw attention to this fact in your initial conversations. This will establish your background and immediately remove any assumptions about your nationality and how you should be expected to behave.

3 | *After Hours*

During dinner, Asians become more relaxed and like to drink a lot. There's this ritual of filling your cup and you have to drink it up. And then, as gesture of courtesy, you fill their cups and they have to drink them up, and it goes on and on. . . . If I refuse to drink, they become very formal. Most of the time I oblige by taking a small sip; it really helps to loosen up the atmosphere. As a woman, I feel it's important to attend business dinners. It's not necessary to get drunk, but joining in on the festivities is fine. I have found that once I have established my credibility, it stays. (Cupertino, California)

The business day does not end at 5 P.M. in Asia. Dinner and after-hours entertainment are important parts of doing business and establishing and reinforcing business relationships. Women should plan to join business dinners. After that you can use your best judgment as to which other activities you wish to attend. If you decide not to join the additional after-hours activity, you won't miss out on any business-related discussions, since this socializing is mostly for relaxing and for people getting to know each other better on an informal level.

After-hours activities differ somewhat from country to country. In Singapore, for example, dinner usually suffices, and additional entertainment is usually not suggested. In Taiwan, Korea, and Hong Kong, additional entertainment may be provided. This may range from drinking and singing in a karaoke bar to bar-hopping or visiting a hostess bar. This last activity usually includes the companionship at your table of an attractive young woman who will pour your drinks, make conversation, and perhaps, for men, even offer some sexual gratuities. It is understood and often expected that women do not participate in these "men only" activities, where business is rarely discussed.

As a woman, you can accomplish your core relationship-building during dinner and feel comfortable about leaving afterward, using a polite excuse such as having to make a phone call or send a fax or that you have jet lag. However, now that Asian hosts are becoming more accustomed to female business visitors, they may suggest a harmless evening at a karaoke bar where you sing along with music videos. Even then, you still have the option to bow out if you don't wish to be put on the spot and have to sing in front of your colleagues. Our recommendation is to ask in advance about where the group is going, gauge the quality and depth of the relationship you have established with your hosts, and then decide what you want to do. The key message here is that no matter what you decide to do afterward, you should always plan to attend the dinner.

Following are some general observations and guidelines that may be of help. Since customs vary somewhat in each of the Four Tigers, refer also to Chapter 5, "Dining," and the individual country chapters.

BUSINESS DINNERS

In Asia

After the business day is over, there will usually be a business dinner. It is important that you participate, since the dinner is an extension of the business meeting and continued business discussions may take place there. The more relaxed atmosphere at the dinner venue will help nurture your relationship with your Asian business peers and build trust.

When your trip or negotiations have come to a close, it is customary to be invited to a thank-you dinner. Do not be intimidated by the rigid Asian protocol for banquets and business meetings. While it is helpful to have a grasp of Asian etiquette, the important thing is to be polite and cooperative and to demonstrate goodwill. If in doubt, follow Western etiquette. You do not have to apologize for your non-Asian manners, but your guests will appreciate your sincerity if you display knowledge of or interest in the way they do things.

At a Chinese-style banquet, guests are usually seated at a round table, with the chief guest to the left of the host. In ancient days, people would carry their swords in their right hands. The host demonstrated his trust and goodwill toward his guest by seating the chief guest on the left, which gave the guest the advantage should a fast-draw swordfight ensue. These days, not everyone observes traditional protocol, so in all cases you should follow the lead of your host. Chinese hosts will often accompany each guest to the door when a meal or party ends. High-ranking guests may be accompanied to their automobiles and the host may wait until they drive away before going back inside.

Toasting occurs in all cultures, but is more frequent during formal Chinese dinners, where there may be a series of prompted toasts. If you are the guest of honor, you should make the first toast. Prepare one beforehand; do not defer the honor to another colleague.

Korean customs are similar to those of Japan. Dinners are long and often quiet. Tables are rectangular or square, with the host at the center and the other guests seated around him. The guest of honor or highest-ranking guest is seated across from the host; the ends of the table remain empty. Generally, only one toast is offered at the beginning of the meal. Koreans also accompany their guests out to their automobiles.

> Follow basic etiquette. Wait for the host to signal the beginning of the meal before you begin eating. For example, pass the bread and butter around to your guests, unless it is placed within easy reach on the table. When you take a pat of butter, don't try to cut it into a smaller portion before you put it on your plate. Break your bread and eat it in small pieces rather than trying to wolf down a whole piece at once. Don't reach across the table for anything—ask that it be passed to you. Never push your plate to the center of the table when you are finished. Excuse yourself to blow your nose—don't do it at the table or in sight of the other diners. Refrain from chewing gum.

In Your Home Country

When Asian businessmen visit Western companies, they expect to receive the same degree of hospitality they offer Westerners in Asia, and they feel disappointed if it is not forthcoming. In the interest of establishing and nurturing good relationships, try to fulfill their expectations. If you are the female host, be sure to host the business as well as the social functions. Handle everything from the business meeting to the check for the dinner

Asians will often include many people at business dinners as a sign of welcome and respect for their guests. When hosting Asians, it is a good idea to do the same. Learn in advance how many Asian guests you will be hosting, and try to ensure a balance on your side by including other business colleagues. If you can, it is best to match title for title, rank for rank. If you cannot, then having enough people to match the number of guests is better than an uncomfortable imbalance.

Usually the host will start the conversation and the highest-ranked guest will respond. During very formal occasions, only the highest-ranked member of each side will speak. If you are the host, keep the dinner conversation positive and avoid debate. Initiate lively and timely topics such as current events, particularly if they involve your visitors' country.

Take the initiative to ensure that your guests are well taken care of. Asians usually make few requests; however, they generally expect their host to initiate activities and to see to their needs. Accordingly, you should ask what their plans are, what they hope to see and do while they are visiting, and if there is anything special they want to accomplish before they leave, like seeing a renowned tourist attraction or shopping for souvenirs.

If you have the time and inclination, try to socialize after hours with your guests. It's a generous touch and will enhance your relationship. For example, a golf or tennis game might be appreciated, or a shopping or sightseeing trip.

Try to arrange one outing to show that you care about the well-being of your guests. If you can't go along with them, provide a list of things to see, places to go, and restaurants to try or, better yet, arrange a sightseeing excursion for them. Your efforts will be appreciated and reciprocated.

> If you are hosting a meal, learn your Asian visitors' tastes and requirements beforehand. If they have been traveling for some time, they may be ready for their home cuisine. If they are visiting for the first time, they may have a specific meal in mind they would like to try, perhaps one that they can't get at home.

➤ If you are hosting a group, be sure to select a restaurant that can accommodate it, preferably in a quiet location. If you frequent a certain restaurant and establish a rapport with the manager there, you are more likely to be better taken care of.

➤ Don't skimp on the meal. Take your guests to a quality restaurant that has good service, a pleasant atmosphere, and a wide selection of dishes from which to choose.

➤ Asians are uncomfortable about a woman paying. You can handle payment by setting up an account, arriving early, and arranging to pay by credit card, or by excusing yourself discreetly from the table to pay the tab. Avoid having to pick up the bill at the table or pay in view of your Asian guests.

➤ Make your reservation as early as possible and reconfirm it the day before the meal, reiterating your requirements to ensure that the location of the table and its setting are suitable.

➤ It is best to accompany your guests to the restaurant and make sure that after dinner they secure a cab or catch the right bus or train. Formal etiquette advises that you make sure your guests get comfortably all the way back to their hotel.

➤ If your guests bring coats, pay any coat-check fees for them.

➤ If your guests seem unsure about what to order from the menu, make some recommendations; they will be grateful for your advice.

➤ Ask your guests for their preference in beverages, such as Scotch or beer; if they do not order drinks before dinner, we recommend that you order both white and red wine and arrange to have the bottles replaced as they are drunk.

➤ Order last and be served last if you are the host. This will cue the waiter that you are hosting the meal.

➤ If the meal includes any shared dishes, begin passing them to your guests counterclockwise around the table.

➤ Have someone in the host group closest to the drinks refresh them for your guests.

➤ Be prepared to start a conversation about local events, sports, or other current topics of interest. In Asia, the host generally initiates the conversation, so your guests may sit quietly waiting for you to start.

➤ To encourage your guests to talk, ask them open-ended questions, such as questions beginning with the Five W's: who, what, where, when, why.

➤ As host, it is your job to initiate the drinking and eating. You can make a toast, or pick up your fork and encourage your guests to enjoy the food.

ENTERTAINMENT

After Dinner

Once the dinner is over, you may be invited to go out to a drinking establishment, karaoke bar, or hostess bar. You do not have to attend if you think you will feel uncomfortable.

Asian businessmen seldom involve their wives in their business dinners. On the very rare instance that you are invited to a businessman's home, the wife will generally only serve the meal and join in any conversation at that time, but will otherwise remain in the kitchen or another part of the house.

If you do decide to participate in the evening entertainment, remember that you have been entrusted to represent your firm, so maintain your professionalism, both during the day and at night. Westerners are often unaware that Asians see them first as representatives of their company and second as individuals. Before you speak or act, remember that if you engage in derogatory, rude, or lewd behavior, it will be associated directly with your company.

If you are alone, ask the hotel concierge to suggest the best places for you to dine on your own. He or she will, of course, recommend the hotel dining facilities but will usually be able to suggest other options. This is a good time to explore the cultural aspects of the country you are visiting. In each of the Four Tigers you can readily find night tours, dinner shows, and cultural events that can be booked through your hotel. Tours are usually available in English.

Team Tactics

Stick with your team. It is customary in all Asian companies to arrange entertainment for male executives at the end of business days and on weekends. This can be a problem for businesswomen. Sometimes the host is unsure about what to do for his female business guests, so he may include them in shopping or sightseeing trips arranged for the business wives, while the men are invited to play golf, fish, or have lunch or dinner together. While he may be thinking about your comfort from his vantage point, you would be in a better position if you could network with your male business counterparts.

The rule of thumb on this, as businesswomen have advised, is to turn down outings planned for the wives unless you really love shopping, have a close relationship with the wives of your team members, or feel you might put yourself in an embarrassing position if you accepted, for example, a golf date and don't play golf. If you want to participate in golf or another sport, make sure you are good at it so that you won't slow the others down or make your host feel uneasy about having to watch out for your safety and enjoyment. Accordingly, if you are the only beginning golfer invited, it is best to politely decline. If your whole team is invited, you are all beginners, and your hosts are willing to put up with all of you, then by all means go.

Find out what activities the group will and will not participate in before you go out for the evening. Your team may be taken to a karaoke bar where there are MTV-like video tapes with words to sing along to. Some places have X-rated videos, subdued lighting, accommodating hostesses, and plenty of liquor. Not everyone appreciates this form of entertainment. The team leader can help set the tone for the group by selecting appropriate activities in which everyone can participate. Help your hosts by suggesting places of interest and after-hour activities that can be enjoyed by all.

If you elect to go out as a group, remind your male colleagues to assist you if the social situation should begin to get out of hand. Ask them, for example, to redirect conversations that are becoming too personal or are inappropriate. Similarly, women can assist male colleagues who may be challenged to drink excessively or who are set up with a woman for the night by reminding them that they represent their business and, as such, should maintain their professionalism.

Should the drinking appear to be getting rowdy, team leaders can bow the team out by offering a business-related excuse, such as that there is a meeting they need to attend or phone calls they must make. Excuses are perfectly acceptable as a polite way of saving face.

If a team member wants to leave during the evening, a business-related excuse or personal excuse like having jet lag, will help him or her bow out gracefully. The host's initial reaction will most likely be to end the activity. If the rest of the group wants to stay, help your departing team member call a taxi and let the host know that you would like to stay for a while longer.

Basic Strategies for After-Hours Entertainment

➤ The business day extends over dinner, so be sure to attend, even though as a woman you may be expected to decline dinner invitations due to jet lag or fatigue. While business may not be discussed over dinner, the more relaxed atmosphere there will help nurture the business relationship and build trust.

➤ Let your hosts know beforehand if you do not want to participate in a planned after-dinner activity.

➤ If your group would like to go and you do not want to join them, politely bow out.

➤ If you are considering entertaining after dinner, some appropriate venues are local tourist spots, tourist lounges, popular shows or concerts, and bus or minivan tours of the area. If you choose a show, make sure your guests will be able to understand it.

For Women Only

➤ If you are (or were) married, use Mrs. before your name, even if you don't at home. Ms. is not often used in Asia, so single women are generally referred to as Miss.

➤ If you are single, avoid talking about your personal lifestyle or dating, as these subjects can lead to uncomfortable conversations. In particular, do not discuss your marital situation if you are divorced or living with someone.

> If you feel that a conversation is inappropriate, don't respond or change the subject.

> Avoid situations where any unwanted intimacy may be initiated, such as dinners for two.

> Be careful that your actions cannot be interpreted as being either aggressive or flirtatious.

> If your Asian guests insist on following Western etiquette by opening doors for you or holding your chair at the dining table, graciously allow them do so. Remember they are trying to respond appropriately when working with Western women.

> If you are in a social setting that is becoming uncomfortable, politely request that your host assist you in getting a taxi. If he does not cooperate, ask the establishment's staff to call one for you.

> Avoid eating or drinking alone in unknown restaurants, since you may be viewed as a pick-up target. Hotel restaurants are considered the safest.

> If you choose to entertain at home, we recommend using a catering service so that your work role is not confused with a domestic role. Use your discretion about inviting guests to your home, based on the relationship you have established with them. If you are single, don't entertain an all-male guest list at home.

> If you are the female host in your home country, select an appropriate restaurant that complements your company, rank, and title. Over time, establish a rapport with the maître d' there to make sure your needs are met and to bolster your credibility with your guests.

Responding to Uncomfortable Questions

When you are asked an uncomfortable or inappropriate question, use short, standard answers to discourage further questioning. For example, the question "Why don't you have any children?" can be answered simply by saying, "Someday." You may also choose to remain silent, or politely change the subject.

If you are posed with an aggressive question such as "Do you want to have sex with me?" be assertive and answer, "This is not an appropriate question to ask" or, if the questioner is being uncooperative, force a loss of face by telling another party about your discomfort. You might ask, "Is it appropriate for people of your culture to ask these questions of professional women?" Silence can also be very effective. If you simply ignore the question and change the subject, the questioner may take it as a subtle hint not to proceed any further. (See Chapter 4, "Sexual Harassment," for advice on specific situations.)

KARAOKE BARS

Socializing and singing together at a karaoke bar is a good way to further enhance the business relationships in Asia. The recent popularity of these bars worldwide suggests that this is not only an accepted method of entertainment, but also one that all cultures enjoy. Karaoke bars are usually in nightclub style, offering either private rooms where groups can sing together, an open lounge area where groups can sit together and sing, or an open bar format where people get up in front of the whole group and sing. The music is usually canned, with video accompaniment in the form of mood images and subtitled lyrics for the viewer to follow. Some karaoke bars offer live music. Each group or customer is given a book that has a list of songs, generally popular Asian and Western tunes, that can be requested. Some of our respondents, however, didn't like the idea of having to sing in front of their business associates, managers, or subordinates. And many Western women will find some karaoke bars just plain unacceptable due to the off-color behavior, the fawning hostesses, and the visually shocking nudity on the karaoke videos.

Love It
I love to sing and really enjoy going to a karaoke bar with my clients. I feel it's one of those rare opportunities to establish a relationship with complete strangers. I have always had positive, wholesome experiences. It is so much better than bar-hopping. (Atlanta, Georgia)

Not My Style
I feel uncomfortable singing in a karaoke bar in front of people I know on a professional level. When the option comes up, I usually decline, stating I have other business to attend to. (Boston, Massachusetts)

Feeling Inhibited
I hate singing. I have a lousy voice. I have a low-pitched voice and can't sing those high-pitched songs. I do go along, but then usually say that I am too shy to sing. I want to stay with the group, but they haven't been able to get me to sing. Maybe one day. (New York, New York)

Mouth Along
I'm too embarrassed to sing. I go out with the group because I know everyone enjoys singing. When push comes to shove, I make sure I get at least four other people to sing with me and then I end up mouthing the songs anyway. At least I try and I know my hosts usually appreciate my efforts. (Phoenix, Arizona)

Take a CD
Karaoke is popular all over the world. I find it embarrassing to sing, but just decided one day to take the bull by the horns. I went out and bought a karaoke CD, the kind you practice with at home. I played it every day in my car until my trip, and then brought it along with me. When my turn came, I handed them the CD and said "play this song; it's the only one I know." At least I could sing one song and everyone was happy with it. (Los Angeles, California)

Tackle It As a Team
No one on my team likes to sing. I think it was mostly because it was new for us. So I had a team off-site where we went to a karaoke restaurant afterward and just agreed to let loose in front of each other. The purpose was to practice together and get the hang of it. We had such a good time. Once everyone got over their inhibitions and stagefright, we actually got some good solos, duets, and group songs together. We were well prepared for our trip. (San Francisco, California)

Coaxed by a Friend
One of my very close Asian friends took me out to a karaoke bar. He knew how embarrassed I was about having to sing on my upcoming trip. He basically said he would keep singing and I could join in whenever I got comfortable. After a while I got the hang of it. I can't say I'm any good, but I had a lot of help from the staff at the bar. (Sunnyvale, California)

Basic Strategies for Karaoke Bars

Here's the best of the advice we gleaned from our interviews:

➤ Get a karaoke CD or tape and practice one song before you go. Bring it with you and, when your turn comes, request that it be played.

➤ Go to a local karaoke lounge and practice with your business colleagues or friends before your trip. This may be all you need to get over the stagefright and realize that you have a presentable voice.

➤ Encourage a group song. You can always just mouth the words; it is the group participation that counts.

➤ Pick an easy song to sing like "Jingle Bells." It is short and has very little variation, so it's good for just about all voice ranges.

➤ Get creative and talk or chant a song instead of singing. Good ones to try for this are "Walk on the Wild Side," or "New York, New York."

➤ After you hear a few others sing, you will realize that very people few sing well, so you might as well join in.

4 | *Sexual Harassment*

Sexual harassment happens. Usually it involves the boss and his secretary or one of his staff members. He will take advantage of her because of his position. There is no way for her to make it stop; she would have to leave the company. You may think we are a non physical culture, but this is not true. Sexual harassment and touching happen out of sight and behind closed doors. (Taipei, Taiwan)

Sexual harassment occurs in the Asian workplace just as it does in the West. Unfortunately, there is as yet little legal recourse available in Asia. The Westerner in Asia may unwittingly and unavoidable be party to conversations and actions that discriminate against women. It is natural in Asian businesses, for example, to ask a female employee to serve tea. A woman may hear perfectly innocent questions about her age, marital status, or whether or not she has children. In Korea, which is generally considered to be the most discriminatory country in Asia toward women, protocol, as in Japan, has men entering rooms and elevators ahead of women.

Sometimes, however, you may observe or be party to actions that go beyond discrimination, such as offering business to a salesperson in exchange for sexual favors. Western women traveling in Asia are not immune to sexual harassment. Therefore, it is important that you understand Asian culture and be able to distinguish culture-based gender discrimination from sexual harassment, and act accordingly.

It is also important for you, your team, and your managers to understand the strategies you should pursue if you find yourself in a compromising situation. Managers should be well versed about their responsibilities in cases where women have been harassed, and they should understand how to act in accordance with company policy and governing laws. For example, an executive team based in the home office in the United States is nevertheless legally responsible for the actions of their employees worldwide.

THE ASIAN POINT OF VIEW

Asian culture has traditionally placed more value on male offspring and on the male roles of ruler, protector, cultivator, and breadwinner. The male is out in the world, while the female remains at home to manage the household and raise the children. Asian males have consequently been in a dominant position over Asian women and have largely controlled their means of livelihood.

Marriages in Asia were arranged not for love but for family connections. The bride usually lived under the domination of the husband's mother and frequently faced competition from secondary wives and concubines. A wife could be repudiated by her husband for various reasons, especially if she did not produce a male heir. If the husband died, she could not easily remarry. She had no economic independence, was frequently illiterate, and had no property rights. Infanticide limited the number of female children.

Centuries ago, male philosophers, China's elite, developed precepts of behavior, notably passivity and obedience, that women were expected, and forced, to follow. Women were subordinated to their fathers, brothers, husbands, and even sons. Foot binding may have been developed in China as a way to keep women in their place. Confucius, the most influential philosopher, whose precepts form the moral code for many Asian societies, placed husband before wife.

Today, the Four Tiger countries continue to be patriarchal societies with strong Confucian traditions. When a woman marries, she generally joins her husband's family. Her ties with her own family weaken. The couple either lives with the husband's family or, as is occurring more frequently, on its own. If there is a divorce, the father often gets custody of the children. Divorce is considered shameful and is rarely discussed.

Divorce rates, which used to be very low in East Asia, are, however, growing as women become more economically independent.

There is an old Chinese saying: "Women are the moon reflecting the sunlight." Young, educated East Asian women increasingly reject this old saw. They emphasize their individuality, independence, personal responsibility, hard work, and careers even as they try to maintain their femininity. Yet the few recent studies of Asian women indicate that many still feel inferior to men and worry about managing a career and a family. Job discrimination is still practiced in Asia. "Family connections" are very important in obtaining desirable jobs. Stereotyping women as the weaker, less capable sex still prevails.

UNDERSTANDING ASIAN CUSTOMS

As a Western woman it is essential that you refrain from being overly offended by what may seem to be blatant sexual discrimination. Keep the Asian cultural background in mind and you will be able to deal with any possible harassment situations with a cool head.

Most Asian companies that do business with Americans are well aware of the Western business style. Western businesswomen have already established their authority and credibility to the point that most Asians view them as being quite different from their Asian sisters. This is to our advantage, since we are expected to behave differently. Non-Asian women of Asian ancestry, however, find it more difficult to establish their authority. Asian men still view them as Asian women and psychologically assign them the traditional woman's role.

But this situation is changing. As more women enter the work force in Asia, they not only are acquiring more money but are assuming more influence in the marketplace. Advertisers and marketers have begun to direct more of their efforts to the female Asian consumer. Many banks in Asia, for example, aware of the purchasing power of working women, now offer women-only credit cards.

DEALING WITH SEXUAL HARASSMENT

Working in the international arena can be tough. Many foreign countries have no laws or regulations concerning sexual harassment and so do not understand the Western viewpoint. As a result, male managers in the West who are unfamiliar with Asia may avoid sending female staff members to represent their companies because they don't think women can be effective in male-oriented societies. This viewpoint, however, may be keeping these executives from using what is in fact their strongest asset, since women's perceived attributes of being good listeners, mediators, and consensus builders are well received in Asian business sessions. Male managers only need to become knowledgeable about the situation in Asia and what their responsibilities are in the event of sexual harassment. They can then send their female staff members with confidence.

U.S. courts and companies offer some legal, preventative back up for discrimination and harassment situations: "The [U.S.] courts have established that corporations that assign a U.S. citizen to a post in a foreign country must treat that person as if he or she were in the U.S., regardless of local customs and traditions. Recent Supreme Court cases suggest several legal/human resource strategies that could be used to prevent gender discrimination . . . [such as to] educate and prepare employees sent to work in different countries abroad. Should a dispute arise, arbitration or mediation is preferred over litigation. The best overall strategy is to develop and implement a well-conceived [company] policy that ensures gender equality."[1]

Management Responsibility

The elimination of sexual harassment starts at home. If your company doesn't have a company policy on discrimination and sexual harassment at home there will be little to back you up if you find yourself facing such situations in Asia. Top management must therefore first take a proactive role in eradicating it from the workplace. There are many good reasons for doing so. Sexual harassment can reduce employee productivity and morale. Consequently it can have a negative impact on a company's bottom line, as well as cost everyone a great deal in lawsuits.

Top management must instruct its staff that sexual harassment is illegal and will not be tolerated. It is the responsibility of the executive staff to eliminate it. Issuing sexual harassment policies, scheduling open discussions, expressing disapproval, creating a path for resolution and complaint, and respecting individual privacy should all be part of the top management plan. A comfortable environment with open, companywide communication is key to alleviating any inhibitions employees may have about discussing their experiences.

If you are in management, you can play a key role. Do not overlook or refuse to acknowledge that problems can also occur overseas, because this will only help reinforce their acceptance. If one of your traveling staff is harassed, it will interfere with the productivity of your business dealings. Harassment also violates U.S. law. It is frustrating for an individual who has faced sexual harassment to work with or for staff who do not understand the seriousness of the offense or travel with a manager who does not speak or act on behalf of employees.

As a first step, a company needs a visible, comprehensive policy emphasizing the importance of appropriate behavior: harassment and social misconduct toward its employees will not be tolerated. This policy should also state the ramifications of any violations. Hard copies of the company policy should be distributed not only internally but also to customers and suppliers. A copy of the policy should be available to all employees and visibly posted in work spaces and rest areas. The company should have training programs for its management staff and its employees on a regular basis.

Individual Responsibility

Prepare yourself for the possibility of encountering sexual harassment when you travel to Asia. Although you are visiting countries that are male dominated and still have little awareness of women's rights, your actions can have a greater impact on men in Asia than at home. In general, Asian men are less assertive and vocal than their Western counterparts. If they commit what is seen by a Western woman as an inappropriate remark or action, their behavior can usually be stopped. Strongly voice your disapproval and the men will often back down. They don't want to lose face by offending you.

In Asia, women often find that while their business days go smoothly, it is the after-hours socializing that becomes a challenge. It is still common for Asian men to go out drinking after work. While drinking, they feel more comfortable about voicing their inner feelings. If you are the lone woman in your group, you may become the target for questions that would not be asked during working hours. In Asia, drinking excuses what Westerners may consider appallingly inappropriate behavior. While the Westerner may remain upset if he or she feels anything untoward has occurred during an evening, the incident is generally ignored by the Asian participants the next day, when it becomes business as usual.

Should you be subjected to what you feel is sexual harassment, remain calm and professional. This attitude will have much more impact than if you become upset or angry. Asian men may have been baiting you to either incite you or test your resilience. In Asia you can either respond with a calm statement of disapproval, or you can show your disapproval by remaining silent. If the situation becomes particularly unpleasant, you can always leave.

There are two types of sexual harassment defined by U.S. law: quid pro quo and hostile environment. Quid pro quo means that an employee is asked to perform a sexual act in exchange for a job, promotion, or other perk. Hostile environment is described as situations, acts, or items that can inhibit the productivity of an employee, such as sexually suggestive language, behavior, or pictures. Some strategies for employees who experience sexual harassment include confronting the individual by informing him or her of the intrusive behavior and requesting that he or she stop it, notifying management, or, should management be the offender, notifying your personnel department or EEOC representative.

If you are traveling overseas on business and have been accosted, you are still protected as an employee of a U.S. firm, and should take action in accordance with your firm's sexual harassment policy.

CASE STUDIES

Obnoxious Behavior
Our Korean supplier came to visit us in the U.S. for the first time. It was agreed that we meet at a restaurant. I was unfamiliar with the protocol and my male team members just asked me to show up if I wanted to. Since I was new to the team and to the supplier, I felt I should go. When I arrived, I was asked to sit at the end of the table since the engineers who had established friendships with the group wanted to sit with their

Korean buddies. As it turned out, I was seated next to men who drank and smoked a lot. They became quite obnoxious toward me during the meal, continuously asking personal questions about my age, my marital situation, boyfriends, etc. They even asked me about my sex life! This made me feel extremely uncomfortable, particularly because no one else at the table was listening to this discussion. They were engrossed in telling jokes for old time's sake. I told my manager back at work how uncomfortable and violated I felt. He shrugged and said, "Next time don't go." (Los Angeles, California)

MANAGER STRATEGIES

➢ When such an incident occurs, the victim's situation should be viewed seriously and her concerns treated as valid. The manager should ask the employee what actions she feels would help her in this situation and in the future to avoid similar incidents.

➢ The manager can then take immediate action by contacting the offender and stating that the behavior was inappropriate and unacceptable to individuals in his group and firm.

➢ The manager should send a copy of his company's sexual harassment policy to the individual. If there is no company policy, the manager should urge the company to produce one and issue it to its business partners worldwide.

➢ The manager and the entire team should discuss appropriate behavior toward the colleague, who was new to Asian business and the team, and how they can become stronger as a team by including all members in the dinner discussions.

➢ In the incident cited above, the woman met with resistance from her management. Therefore, she should discuss her concerns with the manager. If the situation is not successfully resolved, she should report her concerns to her personnel department, the manager's superior, or any other manager who has the responsibility to take action.

INDIVIDUAL STRATEGIES

➢ If you find yourself in a similar situation, you can vocalize your concerns, politely but assertively, directly to the offenders at the table, by telling them their conversation is inappropriate. Then change the subject.

➤ You can shame the offenders and cause them to lose face by letting other people at the table know that the conversation is uncomfortable for you.

➤ You can politely move, if you feel this would terminate the unwelcome activity. A sensitive way would be to say that the smoke is bothering you and you would prefer to sit at the other end of the table. More assertively, you can say that you would prefer to have a more appropriate conversation with other members at the dinner table, because the conversation has become uncomfortable.

➤ You can leave. Tell the group why you are leaving and what behavior is bothering you that is causing you to leave.

Privacy Violated

While I was on a business trip to Singapore, one of the local vendors hosted me and my teammates to an opulent crab dinner. At the dinner, the host asked me where I was staying. I hesitated to answer, but a male teammate at the table did so for me. Though annoyed, I dismissed it since there was a woman sitting with the host whom I thought was his wife. The following morning, I received an early call from him asking me to go to his home to finish our meeting and go swimming. I was suspicious and told him I was married and declined. He responded that he didn't care if I was married or single. He further stated that I should not care either, that I should just enjoy Singapore and him and that it would foster very good business relations. I felt uncomfortable that he had added the business element to his personal agenda; I felt he was playing on the business aspects to get me to comply. I felt really embarrassed about this situation and told my manager about it. My manager was shocked about this behavior and said it couldn't possible happen in "sterile" Singapore. . . . I must have misunderstood his intentions. (Seattle, Washington)

MANAGER STRATEGIES

➤ The manager should take action on the violation of this woman's privacy, since such incidents can occur anywhere, even in "sterile"

Singapore. One approach would be for the manager to contact the individual and suggest that his behavior was unacceptable to his team and company. The manager should also work with his team to heighten awareness about similar situations that could arise when they are traveling overseas.

➤ The manager can initiate a team meeting with employees to investigate strategies and responses for similar situations that may arise overseas and how to work together to strengthen the team.

➤ In the incident cited above, the woman met with resistance from her management. Therefore, she should discuss her concerns with the manager. If the situation is not successfully resolved, she should report her concerns to her personnel department, the manager's superior, or any other manager who has the responsibility to take action.

➤ All team members must be reminded that no one is to give out personal information about somebody else to anyone, including the name of the hotel or phone number of the place they are staying, without that person's express permission.

INDIVIDUAL STRATEGIES

➤ If you find yourself in a similar situation, you can advise your colleagues that you are feeling uncomfortable about a certain individual and ask them to not give out any personal information, such as where you are staying.

➤ A polite but firm no is an appropriate response to any individual who makes offensive suggestions.

Lewd Sing-Along Videos

After dinner while in Hong Kong, I was taken to a karaoke bar with my male colleagues and a director. I was the only woman in the group. Since I did not know what karaoke was, it seemed harmless and "the thing to do" after dinner. They showed us American and Asian rock videos to sing along with at the bar. Well, the Asian videos became very X-rated and I did not know what to do. My male colleagues were in as much shock as I was. I mentioned to my manager, who was there, that I was pretty uncomfortable and wanted to leave. He didn't seem to know what to do either. It was evident that we were all very uncomfortable, but it was also obvious that no one knew how to handle the situation for fear of insulting our counterparts. (Austin, Texas)

MANAGER STRATEGIES

➤ The manager could ask that no X-rated videos be played or suggest that it is time to end the evening.

➤ The manager could explain to the hosts that X-rated video karaoke is inappropriate entertainment for his company group and that perhaps they could continue the evening elsewhere.

➤ The manager should send a copy of his company's sexual harassment policy to the host company. If there is no company policy, the manager should urge the company to produce one and issue it to its business partners worldwide.

➤ In the incident cited above, the manager was unsure about how to respond in an awkward situation. Therefore, the woman should discuss her concerns with the manager. If the situation is not successfully resolved, she should report her concerns to her personnel department, the manager's superior, or any other manager who has the responsibility to take action.

INDIVIDUAL STRATEGIES

➤ If you find yourself in a similar situation, you can request that the videos be changed. Clearly state that you find the videos offensive so that everyone will understand that they are inappropriate.

➤ You can enlist the help of your colleagues to encourage your hosts to change the videos, or you can all leave the establishment together.

➤ You can leave, after telling the host and your manager that you find the videos offensive.

Karaoke Come-On

When I am in Taiwan, we like to go out for a big Chinese dinner. Then cars arrive after dinner to take us to another place for an after-dinner activity. This particular time, the hosts decided that we would go to a karaoke bar. I figured it would be like the karaoke bars in the U.S. They ushered us into a private room and numerous hostesses were ushered in as well. They knelt next to each one of us on the floor. They played video songs and started to sing. The drinking that had started at dinner continued. The lights soon dimmed and the women started heavily necking and petting with the men. I was flabbergasted and so were my American male colleagues. To top it off, one of the hosts felt it was okay to invade my space and come on to me! I politely informed him that I had had enough and perhaps he could assist me with a taxi. I stood up and motioned to leave. He felt obligated at that point to break up the evening, which relieved most of my colleagues. He was very angry with me though, and I started to worry about how it would affect our business relationship. I felt violated, as did my colleagues. Since I was the only woman and no one else seemed to have enough nerve to intercede or stop the behavior, I felt I had to do so. (Sacramento, California)

MANAGER STRATEGIES

➤ A follow-up phone call should be made by the manager to the hosts stating that the behavior toward the employees of the firm was felt to be inappropriate. A phone call from management also reinforces that what the employee did was appropriate and that the behavior exhibited is not acceptable to the firm.

INDIVIDUAL STRATEGIES

➤ In this case, the woman took the appropriate action.

Stalked to the Hotel

I often travel to Korea alone. I generally meet my team at the airport and take a bus to the downtown hotels. On one trip, a middle-aged Korean client met me at the airport saying he was going to escort me to my hotel. He asked where I was staying and said he was going to stay there too. But the way he said it felt very uncomfortable. It started to get obvious that maybe he had another agenda. He seemed like a very respectable, harmless type. He then asked me if I was married. I obviously was wearing a wedding ring and nodded yes. Then he asked me if I had a good marriage, to which I said, "Yes, of course." He went on fur-

ther to say that he did not have a good marriage and that he was available if I wanted to have "really good" fun while I was in town. He continued to ask some pretty prying questions all the way to the hotel, which I duly tried to avoid and change the subject. When we got to the hotel, he followed me up to the desk. It was like he was trying to find out what room I was staying in. Once I got to my room I quickly called down to the desk and asked them to change my room and not let anyone know my new room number. (Detroit, Michigan)

INDIVIDUAL STRATEGIES

➢ Short-term affairs are common in Asia. While Asian men are generally reserved, you may meet an assertive man who wishes to test his luck with a Western woman. Changing the topic or failing to respond to his questions or comments is a good way to demonstrate your lack of interest.

➢ In the incident cited above, the woman changing her room was a good move, since her client was so persistent. In addition to her silence and obvious lack of interest, the room change would probably be sufficient to deter the man.

➢ If the situation continues, the woman should ask her management to send a letter or make a phone call stating the inappropriateness of the man's behavior and the discomfort it caused her and thus the whole group.

Racy Calendar Gifts

Every year our Asian counterparts send us little holiday gifts at the end of the year. For the most part, the items are small, like company logo pens, day timers, or calendars. Every year this Taiwanese firm sends us picture calendars. And every year it is the same thing—nude Asian women in seductive poses. The first year, although surprised, I didn't think much about it. But my male counterparts would relish the arrival of their calendars, gather together, and review them with lots of comments about Miss February or Miss December, etc., and put them up in their offices as a gift. I started to get rather perturbed by this. I asked my manager who was male if there was a way that we could encourage this Taiwanese company to not send these calendars anymore and discourage people from putting them up. He just shrugged and said, "It's a gift, you can throw yours out if you want to." (Knoxville, Tennessee)

MANAGER STRATEGIES

➤ The manager should take this woman's request seriously, since the hanging calendars create a hostile environment for her and possibly other employees. His actions should include talking to employee groups and asking them to remove the calendars to personal environments such as their homes.

➤ The manager should also tell the Taiwanese firm that its gifts, while generous, are not appropriate for his staff and to not send them in the future.

➤ The manager should send a copy of his company's sexual harassment policy to the Taiwanese firm. If there is no company policy, the manager should urge the company to produce one and issue it to its business partners worldwide.

➤ In the incident cited above, the woman met with resistance from her management. Therefore, she should discuss her concerns with the manager. If the situation is not successfully resolved, she should report her concerns to her personnel department, the manager's superior, or any other manager who has the responsibility to take action.

INDIVIDUAL STRATEGIES

➤ The individual was correct to approach her management about her feeling that the calendars created a hostile environment.

➤ If you find yourself in a similar situation, in addition to approaching the manager, you could politely tell your colleagues that you feel the materials are offensive and suggest they be moved to a private, personal area.

➤ If you do not receive your colleagues' cooperation, you can contact your local EEOC office to help you take action.

Verbal Attack

I was on a bus in Korea with my male subordinates and our Korean hosts traveling to visit one of our supplier's factories. The conversation was quite casual and we talked about a lot of things. Then one of the Korean men asked me if I was married and I said yes. He then asked me if I had any children. After I responded to that question in the affirmative, he then asked me how my husband could allow me to travel and conduct business. He continued on a tirade about how the woman's role was in the home and having babies. He further stated that I couldn't possibly be a good mother nor could my husband be a real man! (Tampa, Florida)

INDIVIDUAL STRATEGIES

➤ Koreans may appear to be very macho. Ignore this type of conversation and don't take it personally. Silence is an effective response to any such comments or statements.

➤ This situation would most likely be considered sexual discrimination rather than harassment, but some action might be taken to help diffuse the situation. For example, you could try to change the subject to something more positive or business related.

➤ A more assertive approach would be to state that you feel that these questions are intrusive and insulting and you do not intend to continue discussions along these lines.

➤ Ask your management to send a copy of the relevant parts of your company policy to this individual and his management that include the actions that could be offensive to company employees.

Excluded from Evening Activities

It was my first trip to Taiwan. The group was all men, except for me. I was requested to join this group overseas since I was a key player for their negotiations. The trip was a long one and we were to have numerous meetings and dinners throughout our stay. It became obvious to me that my team members were accustomed to "having a good time" while they were in Asia and were rather uncomfortable traveling with a woman. The dinners we had were formal and in very nice places. Our nights, I felt, were professionally handled and I was enjoying myself. As the trip progressed, it became obvious to me that my teammates were getting annoyed with me for being around. It was obvious that I was stopping some after-hours entertainment that they were accustomed to. Although it was never stated by my colleagues or my hosts, I started to understand. Then one day after a meeting I casually mentioned how tiring these trips were. I initiated the discussion more to find out how my colleagues handled long trips that include long stays and long nights. Then the highest manager in our group surprised me by saying, "Since you are so tired, I will be sure to let our host know that you won't be joining us for dinner tonight. After all, it would be better if you could catch up on your sleep for the rest of our meetings." (Purchase, New York)

MANAGER STRATEGIES

➢ The manager's response was inappropriate. When employees travel overseas, they should remember that they represent the firm and that their business behavior should not change when they are out of their own country. This manager was not well versed in his responsibilities to his firm and its employees.

INDIVIDUAL STRATEGIES

➢ Remind the manager that the dinner is a critical part of the business day and it is important that all team members attend it. Emphasize that as part of the team, you plan to attend the dinner.

➢ You can discuss the points above and indicate that your interest is strictly in business and attending the dinner and that what they do afterward is their business.

➢ If you find yourself in a similar situation, you can continue to join your colleagues for dinner but leave after dinner, which could help relieve the immediate situation.

➢ Upon your return, you could discuss the company's policy on overseas travel, entertaining, etc., with your management and, if there is no policy, ask them to provide one for all employees to follow.

➢ Encourage a discussion with your management and the travel manager about the responsibilities of such managers to protect the overseas teams.

➤ Encourage a discussion among the personnel department, the management, and an employee team about which behaviors are and are not appropriate overseas.

TIPS AND POINTERS

Be Prepared

➤ You may be asked seemingly intrusive questions about your marital status and whether or not you have children. Prepare some stock answers or change the topic of conversation to one that is more comfortable for you.

➤ Entertaining often continues long into the night, so you might be invited to a bar after dinner. Whether or not you want to attend is your choice. It's not impolite to say no, giving jet lag or other business commitments such as faxes or phone calls as an excuse.

➤ Karaoke bars are not the same in Asia as in the United States. Be prepared for X-rated videos, hostesses, sexual remarks, and petting. Have a plan of action to deal with uncomfortable situations should they arise. Let your hosts know in advance, if possible, what situations are offensive to you and your team members to give them an opportunity to change their plans to something more appropriate.

➤ Managers, in particular, should let their hosts know in advance that certain types of entertainment are not appropriate. They can suggest more appropriate activities such as having a drink together in a quiet hotel bar or popular tourist spot.

➤ Have your team decide in advance what actions you will take if one member is uncomfortable with the entertainment. It's easy for the group to say that they have other business to attend to.

Exercise Your Options

➤ If your host exhibits inappropriate behavior, inform him that you are uncomfortable and that you want him to stop.

➤ Get other team members to join you in expressing dissatisfaction with the situation. This will end the unwanted behavior, since to continue it will cause your hosts a loss of face.

➤ If no action is taken, get ready to leave and state the reasons you are leaving. There is no reason to stay in a situation that is uncomfortable for you.

➤ Inform your host that you are uncomfortable and would like to leave. Politely request that he call you a taxi.

➤ An employee who desires to leave while his or her colleagues desire to stay should do so and not feel badly about "breaking up the fun."

EEOC Offices

If you live in the United States you can contact one of the Equal Employment Opportunity Commission's many district or local offices. To find your local listing, phone number, and address, call toll free (800) 669-EEOC. The EEOC will be able to provide you with written guidelines for determining what constitutes sexual harassment and how to deal with it.

WOMEN'S ASSOCIATIONS

If you run into problems in Asia or need advice on how to deal with instances of sexual harassment during your business trip, you may be able to obtain insights and advice from the following organizations:

Hong Kong

➤ **The Hong Kong Association of University Women**
G.P.O. Box 11708
Hong Kong

- President: Ms. Choo-Ai Shaw, Flat 9A, Glendale, 10 Deepwater Bay Drive, Shouson Hill, Hong Kong, Tel: 2574-2326 (work), Fax: 2814-1503 (c/o Mr. Leslie Shaw)

➤ *CIR: Ms. Judy Ng*
G/F, 88 Tai Wai New Village
Shatin, NT
Tel: 2692-4509 or 2788-7220
- Secretary: Ms. Chua Bee Leng, Chinese University of Hong Kong, Shatin, NT, Tel: 2609-7787, Fax: 2603-5104

➤ *The Association for the Advancement of Feminism in Hong Kong*
Room 1202, Yam Tze Commercial Building
17-23 Thompson Road
Wan Chai, Hong Kong

➤ *Hong Kong Council of Women*
GPO Box 819
S 82/F Lai Kwai House, Lai Kok Estate
Kowloon, Hong Kong
Tel: 2728-7760
- Chairperson: Helen Siebers

➤ *Women's Commission*
Asian Students Association (ASA)
511 Nathan Road, 1F
Kowloon, Hong Kong

Taiwan

➤ *The Women's Research Center*
Population Center
National Taiwan University
Roosevelt Road
Section 4, No. 1, Taipei, Taiwan
Tel: (02) 363-0197
Fax: (02) 363-9565
- Coordinator: Dr. Chueh Chang

➤ *The Mandarin Training Center*
National Taiwan Normal University
162 Hoping East Road
Section 1, Taipei, Taiwan

Singapore

➤ *International Business Women's Association*
P.O. Box 23
Orchard Point Post Office
Singapore 9123
Tel: 467-5357
Fax: 467-5357
• Contact: Shantha Farris

➤ *Women's Society of Christian Service, General Conference*
10 Mt. Sophia
Singapore 0922
Tel: 337-5155
Fax: 338-9575
• President: Madame Ing-Eng Wong

➤ *AWARE (Association of Women for Action and Research)*
P.O. Box 244
Tanglin, Singapore 9124

South Korea

➤ *The Korean Association of University Women*
423-44 Ssangmun-dong
Tobong-gu, Seoul 132, South Korea
Fax: (02) 995-7811
• President: Mrs. Yong Un Park, 15-8, Hewha-dong, Chongno-gu, Seoul, South Korea

➤ *CIR: Dr. Uhn-Kyung Choi*
85-203 Banpo Apartments
Banpo Bondong
Seoul 137, South Korea
Tel: (02) 532-4010
• Secretary: Mrs. Soo Hong Kim, HQ

➤ *Korean Women's Development Institute*
C.P.O. Box 2267
Seoul 100, Korea

➤ *FOCUS (Foreigners Community Service)*
- American Women's Club
- Seoul International Women's Association
B5 Namsan Village Apartments
It'aewon-dong
Yongsan-gu, Seoul 140, South Korea
Tel: 798-7529 or 797-8212
- Contact FOCUS for the most up-to-date contacts and phone numbers for women's associations in Korea.

➤ *Korean National Council of Women*
40-427 The 3rd Street
Han River
Yongsan-gu, Seoul 140, South Korea
Tel: (02) 793-5196 or (02) 794-4560
Fax: (02) 796-4995
- President: Mrs. Kyung-O Kim

➤ *Korean Women's Institute*
EWHA Woman's University
11-1 Taehung-dong
Sodaemun-gu, Seoul 120, South Korea
Tel: (02) 360-3224 or (02) 360-3226
Fax: (02) 3123-3625
- Director: Professor Bae Yong Lee

➤ *The National Commission on Women's Policies*
Ministry of Political Affairs
Government Building
77-6 Sejong-no
Chongno-gu, Seoul 110, South Korea

5 | *Dining*

Rice affected by the weather or turned (a man) must not eat, nor fish that is not sound, nor meat that is high. He must not eat anything discolored or that smells bad. He must not eat what has been crookedly cut, nor any dish that lacks its proper seasoning. The meat that he eats must at the very most not be enough to make his breath smell of meat rather than of rice. As regards wine, no limit is laid down; but he must not be disorderly. — The Analects of Confucius

Food and eating are taken quite seriously in Asia. In fact, *Ch'ih-fan le mei-you,* a standard greeting in Chinese, means "Have you eaten?" The idea is that if you have eaten, you must be feeling fine. Foods in Asia are fragrant and attractively arranged, and offer many tasty contrasts—crisp to smooth, spicy to sweet. The most distinctive aspect of Asian cuisines is the attention given to how the food is cut before it is cooked or assembled. Cutting takes on paramount importance to ensure that the presentation and taste are at their best. The aesthetic placement of food on a dish is more important than the size of the serving. Most table settings simply use white china or local pottery.

As a businesswoman traveling to Asia, you will be invited to or will host many dinners. Each of the Four Tiger countries has slightly different menus and dining customs, although Chinese etiquette can generally be followed at Chinese meals and banquets in Hong Kong, Taiwan, and Singapore. Korean food and eating habits merit a separate discussion. We offer the following information to help increase your awareness and enjoyment of Asia's culinary delights. The accompanying notes on eti-quette apply especially to more formal settings, such as banquets or din-ners meant to mark an important business agreement.

HONG KONG AND TAIWAN

There are many styles of Chinese food that originated in different regions of China. The four basic regional types are: Southeastern (Can-tonese and Chaozhou), Northern (Peking and Shandong), Eastern or Coastal (Shanghai), and Southwestern (Szechuan and Hunan). After these four come Hokkien and Hakka cooking styles from southern Chi-na. Areas near the shorelines, such as Shanghai, feature more fish in their dishes, while inland regions such as Szechwan use more spices, which help preserve food. If you plan to host a business dinner in Hong Kong or Taiwan, it is helpful to know that Cantonese cuisine is preferred in Hong Kong and Shanghai cuisine in Taiwan. Taiwan also has a style all its own. Chinese food offers abundant choices for vegetarians.

You may want to ask your Chinese guests to help you by suggesting a balanced menu and an appropriate number of dishes to serve. The bal-ancing of opposing factors such as sun and moon, light and dark, male and female, called *yin* (feminine energy) and *yang* (masculine energy), is a very important Chinese practice. Applied to all areas of one's life, includ-ing food, it is thought to bring about and preserve the harmony of body and mind. In his book *Taiwan*,[1] Daniel Reid says that "During the Tang Dynasty (618–907), it was the Chinese herbal pharmacologists (not the cooks or gourmets) who determined what should and should not be eat-en. They decided what quantities and combinations of food should be prepared and when it should be consumed." Reid describes how an elab-orate system of food pharmacology was developed based on the cosmic theories of yin and yang, and the five elements of earth, air, fire, water, and metal. Yang foods are hot foods that stimulate the body and deplete it of its energies. Yin foods are cool foods that calm and nourish the sys-tem. Neutral foods are a balance of the yin and the yang. For example, whole barley is a neutral food—the yang side heats up the body while the yin side cools the brain. Because a perfect meal contains elements of each and some foods should never be served together, you should always ask your host about the best combinations of foods to order.

Popular Cuisines

Cantonese- and Chaozhou-style food is light, refined, and delicate. Many of the dishes are steamed, boiled, or stir fried. Popular dishes familiar to Western palates include stir-fries, crisp vegetables, steamed fish, and egg rolls. Exotic dishes include ingredients such as snake, birds' nests, sharks' fins, frogs' legs, and turtle.

Ordering *dim sum*, Chinese dumplings, is a good way to sample Cantonese food at brunch or lunch. Carts filled with a variety of steamed and fried dumplings filled with vegetables, shellfish, meat, and sweets are rolled to diners at their tables. You can select whatever dishes look appealing. Five different types of dumplings for lunch would be a satisfying sampling. Delicious dessert dumplings filled with egg custard and sweet beans make a perfect finish for your meal.

Peking and Shandong cuisine is a blend of Mongolian and Manchurian cooking styles that uses generous amounts of wine, garlic, and scallions. Popular Western choices include noodles, pancakes, meat-filled turnovers, and mixed vegetables and meats in sweet and sour sauces. Peking duck, a particular favorite, is roasted duck cut into squares and served in its crisp skin with scallions and a special plum sauce. Tender beggar's chicken got its name from a beggar who supposedly stole a chicken from the emperor and hid it by burying it in the ground to cook it. The chicken is stuffed with herbs, onions, and Chinese cabbage, wrapped in lotus leaves, sealed in clay, and baked all day.

Shanghai cuisine features vegetables and noodles over rice flavored with soy sauce, fresh fish and seafood, especially shellfish, smoked fish, and drunken chicken (chicken cooked in wine). This is the style of Chinese food that many Americans say is on the oily side and too heavy for American palates.

Szechwan and Hunan style dishes are heavily spiced with chili peppers and garlic. Popular Western Szechwan choices are fragrant eggplant, frogs' legs, hot-and-sour soup, and twice-cooked pork. Hunan cuisine includes a variety of seafood, duck, and chicken dishes.

Dishes such as a rice porridge and oysters, mussels, and pork stewed in a rich sauce are native to Taiwan. Other local specialties include oyster omelets, squid balls, fried dried fish, and simmered cuttlefish.

Hokkien or Hakka cuisine, which includes dishes such as steamed chicken and Hokkien fried *mee* (thick egg noodles cooked with pork, seafood, and vegetables in a rich sauce), and Teochew dishes such as

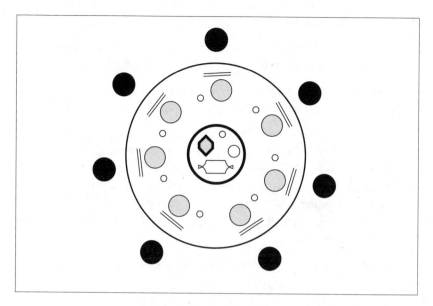

Chinese Seating for Dinner

char kway teow (noodles, clams, and eggs fried in chili and black bean sauce) are very popular in Singapore.

Chinese Dining Etiquette

Chinese tables are most often round, with a rotating server (like a lazy Susan) set in the center. Food is shared. Each diner, who is provided with a small plate or plates, takes food from the dishes on the server and then rotates it to the next person. There can be up to sixteen courses for formal dinners (usually served one dish at a time), and as few as four courses for a simple lunch, generally served at the same time.

The Chinese use chopsticks and a porcelain spoon for the liquid part of the soup. If no special serving utensil is provided for shared dishes, turn your chopsticks around and use the shanks to pick up food to transfer to your plate.

Instead of a napkin, you may be given a damp cloth to clean your hands before and after your meal. Do not use it to wipe your face. Since few restaurants provide napkins, it is wise to carry a handkerchief, tissues, or towelettes.

BEGINNING THE MEAL

➤ If you are the highest in rank or the focal point of the meeting, you will be invited to sit next to the host during the dinner.

➤ Allow your host to select the menu for the table. Because food is shared, do not order one dish just for yourself.

➤ If you are the person ordering the meal, ask your host or waiters to help you. Have them tell you which items are fresh for that day and advise you on what to order. You may get a menu designed for visiting Westerners rather than the local Chinese menu. Order one dish per person in the group, including an appetizer, soup, and a dessert (usually fruit). Keep the yin and yang principles in mind when you make your choices.

➤ There will be some communal dishes and some individual dishes.

DURING THE MEAL

➤ Your host, who is obliged to take care of you, may try to continually refill your plate and rice bowl. Politely refuse when you have had enough. You may have to refuse a few times before your refusal is finally accepted.

➤ Don't rummage through the serving dishes with your chopsticks to get the best morsels, but select the piece closest to you from the dish closest to you.

➤ Do not reach across the table.

➤ When you take food from a serving plate, don't put it straight into your mouth. Transfer it to your own plate first.

➤ Hold your rice bowl fairly close to your mouth when eating rice with chopsticks. Do not, however, hold your bowl near your mouth and use your chopsticks to shovel in the food. While this is okay in casual situations, it is considered unrefined in formal settings.

➤ To eat large pieces of food, raise the piece to your mouth with your chopsticks, bite off a small piece, and return it to your plate. You may, however, prefer to use your chopsticks to break the large piece into smaller pieces first.

➤ If there are bones or shells in your food, put them on a small side plate. If there is no side plate, put them on the table.

➤ Noodles are usually preferred to rice. Rice may or may not be served.

➤ When you serve yourself, don't take the last piece on the dish as it will signal that you have not had enough.

CONCLUDING THE MEAL

➤ The serving of the soup signals the end of the meal.

➤ When you've finished eating, lay your chopsticks neatly on the table.

➤ As is traditional in Asia, your host may seem to apologize for a humble meal. In response, thank him or her for the wonderful food.

➤ At the end of the dinner, the guest of honor rises to graciously thank the host on everyone's behalf.

➤ Typically, the Chinese go home after the meal. The Chinese like to talk during dinner, but do not linger around the table over small talk.

➤ Don't let the meal last over two hours, whether it is served in a restaurant or at home.

➤ Before you leave the country, be sure to invite your hosts out to reciprocate for the dinners or banquets they held for you. Don't provide a more expensive dinner than your hosts did, since this would embarrass them.

Chinese Banquets

➤ Banquets are celebration feasts that last about two hours and are larger and more formal than business dinners.

➤ If you are invited to a formal banquet, it is very important to arrive at the restaurant precisely on time.

➤ If you are the guest of honor at a formal banquet, you will sit to the left of the host.

➤ Cocktails are not served before dinners or banquets, but tea is often poured before the guests are seated.

➤ The host usually selects the foods to be served to the guests and gives them their first servings.

➤ When everyone is seated, the host will offer the guests a welcoming toast.

➤ The host might also make a speech and toast your mutual cooperation. Have some complimentary remarks prepared so that you can respond appropriately.

➤ There is a lot of toasting at Chinese banquets and meals. (See "Chopsticks, Toasting, and Tea," below, for general information.)

➤ At banquets, you will be toasted as the guest of honor. To accept a toast, smile, raise your glass, make eye contact, and down your drink in one swallow. Toasts may be conducted sitting or standing. Follow your host's lead.

➤ Prepare a toast for your hosts. As the guest of honor, you should return a toast. Each member of your group may want to have a toast prepared to say when it is his or her turn.

➤ If someone stands up and toasts another person's health, stand, take your glass in both hands, and say a few kind words.

➤ Warm rice wine called *mao-tai* is often served in small cups. Drink it only when making or receiving toasts.

➤ Women are often excused from participating in the heavy drinking. You can fill your glass with water to participate in the many toasts.

➤ If you are the guest of honor, you are expected to be the first to sample any dish that is served. If you see people waiting, start eating.

➤ Chicken brains are a delicacy, so if you are the guest of honor you may be given the head of any chicken served with the meal.

➤ Soups will be served throughout the course of a formal banquet.

➤ Finish all the rice in your bowl. Feel free to ask for a refill. Leave a little food on each serving dish and on your plate, however, or the host will feel obliged to provide more food.

➤ Additional servings of rice, noodles, or tea brought to the table often signal that the banquet is over.

➤ You may be served a very strong tea in a small cup at the end of a banquet. First take a sip. The tea is then poured onto the serving tray to symbolize the bond between you and the other participants.

➤ After the meal, the honored guest should be the first to leave.

SINGAPORE

Restaurant-hopping, eating, and talking about food are passionate pursuits in Singapore. The small nation's diverse cultural mix of Chinese, Malaysian, Indonesian, and Indian peoples provides a wide variety of culinary choices. Adding to the mix are restaurants specializing in European cuisine and American fast food. At open-air markets called "hawker" centers you can select prepared foods from stalls and have them brought to your table. Popular hawker centers are Newton Circus, the Satay Club, and Cuppage Centre.

Singapore also has many popular indoor restaurants. Chinese food, mainly Cantonese, is very popular. Hokkien and Hakka cooking styles are also well-liked. Since Singapore is surrounded by the ocean, seafood is naturally fresh and abundant. Singaporean seafood centers are quite casual and offer the opportunity for some intriguing dining. At the UDMC Seafood Center, for example, you are given a shopping cart or basket when you enter the restaurant. Then you shop around just as if you were in a grocery store, collecting your desired dinner ingredients from the fish or vegetable sections. At the checkout stand you pay and receive a table number. Within twenty minutes or so the food you picked out yourself is cooked and served to you.

Popular Dishes

One of the most popular Indonesian dishes among Westerners is *satay*, skewers of beef, chicken, or lamb grilled over charcoal and served with spicy peanut sauce. Others include *mee rebus*, thick noodles in a spicy sauce; *nasi goreng*, fried rice topped with meat, prawns, and egg; and *tahu goreng*, deep-fried bean curd with bean sprouts. Javanese cuisine is a combination of foods from the islands of Java, Sumatra, and Madura. Special dishes include *pepesan*, fish or prawns in coconut cream and spices on a banana leaf, and *soto ayam*, clear broth with shredded chicken, sprouts, and transparent noodles.

Malaysian dishes include *satay*, fiery curry prawns, and spiced curried beef in a coconut marinade. *Nonya* is a mix of Malaysian and Chinese cuisine combining Malaysian spices with Chinese noodles. A variety of local ingredients are used, including coconut and chilies.

Indian cuisine includes a medley of curries, tandoori chicken, kebabs, and vegetarian South Indian specialties like *masala dosa*, crisp sourdough lentil pancakes filled with potatoes and onions and served with coconut chutney.

KOREA

Korean cuisine is notably different from that of other Asian countries. It features small portions of fish or grilled meat with a variety of tofu and vegetable dishes that are rich in vitamins and low in calories. The food is generally quite hot and spicy. Seasonings include garlic, chili pepper, scallions, soy sauce, fermented bean paste, red pepper paste sauce, ginger, and sesame oil.

When you are invited to dine in a traditional Korean restaurant, it can be quite a feast. You will most likely be seated on the floor on cushions under a low table. The seating protocol is to kneel on your cushions. Kneeling, with your feet tucked under, is a sign of respect to the elders at the table. In the past, each person sat at their own low table and ate in silence. Today, you will find that most Koreans prefer to eat with others and engage in conversation. A Korean dinner will, however, usually be quieter than a Chinese dinner.

A traditional Korean meal includes foods from five categories. There are (1) two types of soup: *kuk* (with a long "u" sound), which is served individually, and *tchigae*, a kind of communal stew. *Kuk* is usually lighter in taste than *tchigae*. Then there are (2) a fish or meat dish, (3) rice, (4) several side vegetable dishes, and (5) *kimch'i* (usually spelled kimchee in the West), the renowned Korean fermented Chinese cabbage, garlic, and red pepper "pickles." All dishes are placed on the table at the same time rather than served in courses. There will be some communal dishes and some individual dishes. There is no set order in which to eat the food, so you can just select what you want. Some of the food will be served in brass or stainless steel dishes to retain the heat. The utensils used are chopsticks and a large spoon.

Popular Dishes

Pulgogi is strips of beefsteak marinated in soy and sesame sauces, garlic, onions, sugar, and pepper and grilled over charcoal, usually on a grill placed on or set into your table. It is the most popular choice among Westerners, since it is similar in taste to our barbecued spareribs.

Pulgalbi is beef or pork spareribs marinated in soy sauce and grilled like *pulgogi.*

Chapchae is a stir-fried dish of mixed vegetables and shredded beef with soybean noodles.

Kalbitchim is a stew of short ribs, turnips, chestnuts, and mushrooms.

Naengmyon is buckwheat noodles in a cold beef broth of vinegar and mustard.

Pindaettok is a bean pancake snack containing green onions and strips of pork.

Kalbit'ang is spareribs served in a mild soup.

Kuksu-chon-gol is a dish of noodles, meat, and vegetables boiled together at your table in a large metal pan.

Sollongt'ang is a savory stew of meat and vegetables in a beef broth soup.

Yukkae-jang is a spicy soup with chopped beef and vegetables.

Chon-gol is meat, noodles, and vegetables cooked together at the table.

Pibimpap is a popular dish of meat, egg, and vegetables over rice served with a spicy chili paste.

Rosu kui is thin slices of beef cooked in water and then dipped into soy and sesame-oil sauces.

Kalbi kui is beef ribs cooked over charcoal.

Sogum kui is generally a lot like our roast beef. It is seasoned with salt, broiled, and then dipped in sesame oil.

KIMCH'I

Kimch'i is the fermented vegetable pickles that are included with every Korean meal. *Kimch'i* dates back to the seventeenth century, when

Koreans discovered that salt and red pepper could be used to pickle vegetables to store for consumption over the long, cold winters. Today there are over a hundred types of *kimch'i*, with variations based on the vegetable used and the fermentation process. Following are some of the more popular varieties:

Kimch'i (that is, whole cabbage *kimch'i*) is the most common type of *kimch'i*. Chinese cabbages are cut lengthwise into several pieces, soaked in brine, drained, seasoned between layers of leaves, and left to ferment.

Possam kimch'i (wrapped *kimch'i*) is a Chinese cabbage *kimch'i* packaged into neat bundles. Usually a seafood such as shrimp, anchovies, or squid is seasoned and wrapped into these bundles, which are left to ferment.

Paek kimch'i (white cabbage *kimch'i*) is from the southern part of Korea. It is less watery and contains more pickled fish and red pepper than northern-style *kimch'i*.

Oisobaegi (stuffed cucumber *kimch'i*) features cucumbers that are sliced down the middle, stuffed with a mixture of regional seasonings, and left to ferment.

Kkaktugi (hot radish *kimch'i*) uses long, white Korean radishes cut into cubes, seasoned, and fermented.

Ch'onggak kimch'i (whole radish *kimch'i*) is made with Korean radishes that are salted, sprinkled with anchovies and seasonings, and pickled.

Tongch'imi (radish water *kimch'i*) is white radishes rolled in salt. After three days, the salt water is poured into a crock and radish leaves are layered over the top and weighed down. The resulting dish looks like white disks in a bowl of clear liquid.

Nabak kimch'i (water *kimch'i*) contains small pieces of white radish or cabbage pickled in seasoned brine and is usually served chilled. There will be some green or red peppers in the dish for taste.

SIDE DISHES

Tubu (tofu): a soft, white bean-curd dish.

Shigumchi: a vegetable similar to spinach that is served garnished with sesame seeds.

Kim: strips of seaweed fried in sesame oil.

Kongnamul: a bean-sprout dish.

Kong: a bean dish.

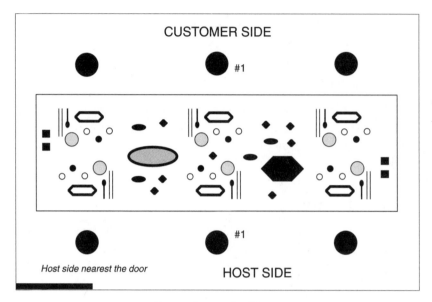

Korean Seating for Dinner

Toraji: a Chinese bellflower root dish.
Yonppuri: lotus root served in a sweet sauce.
Myolchi: anchovies served in a sweet sauce.

Korean Dining Etiquette

Korean dinners are generally much quieter than Chinese dinners or even dinners in Japan. There is less small talk and usually only one toast is made. The person who initiates the meal is assumed to be the host. At traditional meals, you may sit on the floor at a low rectangular table on a cushion. Do not step on the cushion. Women kneel on their knees or sit with their knees tucked under to one side; they do not usually sit cross-legged.

➤ Chopsticks are used and can be bamboo or metal. In local eateries, they will often be the throw-away type. A ceramic spoon is used for soups. Western silverware is used for Western meals.

➤ You will usually be given a hot or cold damp towel with which to wipe your hands before and after meals. Napkins are generally not used.

➤ Before entering a Korean home or a dining room in a Korean restaurant, remove your shoes.

BEGINNING THE MEAL

➤ Unlike Chinese dinners, the Korean meal is generally served all at once. Except for the soup,which is often communal and ladled into small bowls, Korean food is served with a number of individual dishes provided to each person.

DURING THE MEAL

➤ Pour soy sauce into your neighbor's small sauce dish. Your neighbor will do the same for you. In the same way, serve your neighbor tea.

➤ Take the top off your rice bowl and put it on the floor under your place at the table.

➤ Koreans do not lift the rice bowl or any other food bowl off the table when they eat, unlike the Chinese and Japanese. Keep the dishes on the table and bend toward them.

➤ Do not use your hands to pick up any food; instead, invert your chopsticks. Use toothpicks to pick up pieces of fruit.

➤ Pass food with your right hand, with your left hand supporting your right forearm.

➤ People never pour their own drinks. Diners pour each other's drinks and pour refills when their neighbor's glass is empty. Koreans advise that it is not correct for women to pour for other women.

➤ When you pour a drink for someone else, hold the bottle with one hand and support your forearm with your free hand. Usually the left hand is the support hand.

➤ When someone fills your glass, hold it up with your right hand and place your left hand lightly under it.

➤ When you're served tea or coffee, the spoon will be on your side of the cup. After you use the spoon, put it on the side of the cup that is away from you.

CONCLUDING THE MEAL

➤ Do not finish everything served at the dinner. This indicates that you are still hungry, which will imply that your host did not provide enough food.

➤ When you finish eating, lay your chopsticks neatly on the table.

➤ If you are to pay, you may prefer to take care of the bill in advance or at a break, not at the table. In a male-dominated society, it may be difficult for a woman to pay for the business meal, though this is becoming less of an issue in business settings.

CHOPSTICKS, TOASTING, AND TEA

Chopsticks

Chopsticks are used in all Four Tiger countries; however, they differ slightly from culture to culture. Chinese and Korean chopsticks are usually longer than Japanese chopsticks, and blunt-ended rather than pointed. When you are dining in Asia, you may not be offered any Western utensils, so be sure to practice using chopsticks before you go.

HOW TO HOLD CHOPSTICKS

➤ The chopsticks rest in the curvature between your thumb and index finger and are steadied against the ring figure of the same hand. Hold the sticks about two-thirds of the way up. Keep the tips pointed downward toward the table.

➤ The upper stick is held by your thumb, index and middle fingers. The lower stick is held stationary while the upper stick moves to create a pinching effect.

➤ If you lose your grip on your chopsticks by holding them too tightly or too far down, gently tap them on the table to realign your grip.

➤ When you put your chopsticks down, rest them either on the chopstick rest (a small wooden or porcelain piece near your plate) or on the side of your plate.

CHOPSTICK POINTERS

➢ Use serving chopsticks if they are provided. If not and you are selecting something to eat from a platter, turn your chopsticks around and use the shanks to pick up the food.

➢ Never set your chopsticks down parallel on a rice bowl—it's thought to bring bad luck or death to someone at the table.

➢ Do not stand your chopsticks in a vertical position in your bowl—this looks like sticks of incense in a bowl of ashes such as would be seen at a funeral.

➢ Do not spear food with your chopsticks or gesture or point with them.

➢ Do not lick your chopsticks.

➢ Do not cross paths with your neighbor's chopsticks when you reach for food.

➢ Do not take food from another person's chopsticks.

Toasting

Toasting occurs often during Chinese dinners, more so in Taiwan and Hong Kong than in Singapore. Toasts are not as plentiful in Korea. Toasting is a celebration of the time you and your associates have spent together and a time to acknowledge your "friendship" and business relationship. Women who host a dinner or who are guests of honor should initiate or return a toast as required. Do not defer to your male colleagues or pass.

CHINESE CULTURES

➢ At a Chinese meal, the first toast is frequently non-specific, and everyone drinks together. The toasting is usually initiated by the host upon the arrival of the first dish. The guest of honor usually returns the toast. During the dinner, everyone will continue to toast each other.

➤ When you toast in a Chinese culture, hold your cup in both hands.

➤ At Chinese-hosted meals it is the responsibility of the host rather than the waiters to see that the guests' drinking glasses are kept filled. If you do not wish to have your glass refilled, keep it full so that no more is poured in.

KOREA

➤ When you toast with the Koreans, say *kon-bae* ("dry cup") and support your right hand, which is holding the glass, with your left. When a toast is made, both parties are expected to drink.

➤ In Korea, there are generally only one or two toasts at the beginning or end of the meal. If you wish to limit your consumption of alcohol during toasting, fill your glass with water for the toasts. In Korea, diners pour each other's drinks. Watch the glasses and pour refills when your neighbor's glass is empty.

Tea

All Asian countries serve tea at meals. It is said that tea originated in China as early as A.D. 300. Legend has it that an emperor discovered tea when leaves accidentally blew into the water he was boiling. When he went to throw it out, he noticed a fragrant smell emanating from the liquid and, out of curiosity, tasted the brew. Pleased by his new discovery, he shared it with his people.

➤ Chinese tea ceremonies are not as elaborate or formal as those held in Japan. Tea houses are instead local meeting places for friends to talk with each other.

➤ There are three types of tea: green, oolong, and black. All are drunk plain, without milk or sugar.

Refer to the individual country chapters for formal and casual restaurants featuring local and Western cuisines.

6 | *Hong Kong*

I was the sole female visiting a supplier in Hong Kong along with several male colleagues. When I walked into the meeting, a few eyebrows were raised in surprise. There were no problems in the introductions beyond that. What started to bother me the most was the emphasis that our host placed on my gender. He would say, "Gentlemen and lady, please be seated" or "What would the gentlemen and lady like to drink?" or "Would the gentlemen and lady like to join us for dinner?"... Although I was particularly sensitive to the subtle discrimination he was setting up, I chose to ignore it. By the second day, he stopped differentiating me from my colleagues. (Toronto, Canada)

As in most Confucian cultures, women in Hong Kong have long been expected to maintain the traditional roles of wife and mother. During the 1980s, women began to participate more actively in Hong Kong's economic development. Between 1985 and 1989, the number of women entering the work force increased by 8 percent to 36 percent, with more than half employed in the manufacturing sector. Today, half of all women aged fifteen or older are employed, a higher percentage than in any other newly industrialized economy (NIE) in Asia. Women's disposable income has jumped dramatically over the last decade, and with their increased earning power more and more have begun to exert an influence on family purchases. Advertising on Hong Kong TV and radio and in the print media reflects a more assertive Hong Kong woman who keeps her mate waiting and does her own thing. Advertising researchers emphasize however, that Hong Kong women have not completely thrown off their traditional roles, so that the emphasis is still on femininity, whether the image is that of an outgoing, independent career woman or a more traditional wife and homemaker.

In the past, Hong Kong women were designated as second signatories on their husband's credit cards. Now, to lure qualified women to apply for their own cards, some companies even offer free cosmetics. The International Bank of Asia in Hong Kong has gone even farther and introduced "My Card," a women-only credit card that allows women to qualify at a lower salary level than men. This is important, since women's average earnings are only about two-thirds those of men, according to a 1994 study conducted by de Leon and Ho.[1]

Recent studies indicate that "familism" is the most important factor determining whether or not women will have successful management careers. Family ties in Hong Kong are more important than personal goals. Family members are expected to provide mutual assistance. Elderly parents must be taken care of and children nurtured. Spare time is to be spent with families, with social interaction encouraged only if it benefits the family. Marriage and motherhood is considered an honorable occupation offering respect, influence, and love.

Women who want a professional career tend to marry later and have fewer children; almost 28 percent never marry. Since Chinese Hong Kong males tend to marry females with similar educations, families tend to support their daughters in the pursuit of a career. If the daughter never marries, her income becomes part of the family resources. Women who marry look for a "prominent" husband and believe that their role is to support their husbands first. Their own careers come second, according to the de Leon and Ho study.

Women who marry and have a career seek positions with fewer hours. Their children's achievements directly reflect on the family, so they expect to supervise their children's academic pursuits. While some have live-in help, either relatives or paid tutors and caretakers, this, the de Leon and Ho study says, accounts for only 4 percent of dual-income households. As a result, most women tend to be working in lower-level management positions.

The study also found widespread discriminatory employment practices. Males are preferred for managerial positions by a ratio of four to one. Firms recruit women for staff functions, especially in the areas of personnel and public relations. In general, the negative feelings of males toward working women and their reluctance to accept females in supervisory positions continue to impact on the ability of women to advance to line positions. Gender discrimination is not illegal in Hong Kong, and efforts to make it so have been unsuccessful to date. As a result, women appear to be willing to accept lower salaries than men in order to obtain professional positions.

Hong Kong women, however, are becoming increasingly independent and self-assured. They are marrying later and having fewer children. The largest demographic increase of women in the labor force includes those between the ages of twenty-five and thirty-four, the age bracket when most women marry and bear children. As a result, population growth is expected to slow in the 1990s and age rapidly, especially when this is combined with the emigration of young families to other areas of the world as the 1997 return of Hong Kong to China edges ever closer.

Hong Kong women say they are treated with courtesy and respect in business. Their place in the work force is accepted, since it is seen as being a traditional part of the efforts to benefit the family.

DOING BUSINESS IN HONG KONG

Hong Kong businesspeople are often considered abrupt. Hong Kong is a fast-paced financial center, and the behavior of its busy-bee population is not unlike that of New Yorkers. Cantonese is the prevailing language, although Mandarin is understood by many residents and is becoming more popular as Hong Kong nears its return to China.

Hong Kong has been described as an "Oasis in the East." Western women will generally have fewer problems, including credibility problems, working in Hong Kong than in other Asian cities. Hong Kong is the most diverse, most Western, and most familiar environment you will encounter in Asia. Strongly influenced by the British political system and business practices, the city offers few visible traditional barriers for the visitor to overcome. Although predominantly Chinese, the population is diverse, with immigrants and expatriates from many countries.

Hong Kong is a financial mecca and the gateway to China. This wealthy, densely populated island is loaded with imposing skyscrapers, fine restaurants, high-style shops, Rolls Royces, and cellular phones. Some analysts attribute the fast pace of Hong Kong business to the strong, underlying will to survive of the Hong Kong people, who are often said to be living on borrowed time in a borrowed land. For many Westerners, Hong Kong is a capitalist society focused on profit at the exclusion of everything else and regardless of risk.

Hong Kong businesses are diverse. They range from large international companies to traditional small- and medium-sized family-run firms. While the Hong Kong business style is fast paced and focused on money, tradition still plays a role. Many Hong Kong Chinese retain the "owner does it all" mentality. They delegate less than in the West and like to stay directly involved in most business dealings. Relationships and family are of paramount importance. Business is conducted on a face-to-face, one-on-one basis, and only after a relationship has been established.

With women already very visible in the Hong Kong work force, whether at large international firms or small family-run companies, most Western businesswomen report little or no resistance when they are conducting business in Hong Kong. The challenge, they say, is adapting to the results-oriented attitude of the locals and to the hustle-bustle business style.

This was driven home to us during an encounter with a Chinese Hong Kong national we met on a plane. He was married, and both he and his wife worked in management for a large international firm based in Hong Kong. His conversation indicated his preoccupation with making money. He told us how many sleepless nights he had had since he began playing the options market around the clock in the hope of making a lot of money. He was fearful of suffering large losses if he couldn't keep on top of it. He described how he could buy and sell world currency at his local bank using its automatic teller machine. Motivating him was the need for enough money to purchase visas for his wife and her family and finance their move to Australia before 1997, when Hong Kong is returned to China. Hong Kong, he said, was the best place in the world to accrue money quickly, since there is a free flow of currency and opportunities there that cannot be found anywhere else in the world.

HONG KONG IN 1997

Under the terms of a joint 1984 declaration between Britain and the People's Republic of China (PRC) on the question of Hong Kong, currently a self-governing British Crown Colony, Hong Kong will become a Special Administrative Region (SAR) of the PRC in July 1997. It will still have a high degree of autonomy, except in foreign and defense affairs. Current laws in Hong Kong are to remain basically the same for a period of at least fifty years. Private property, business ownership, rights of inheritance, and foreign investments are to be protected by current law, and China has pledged to respect Hong Kong's existing social and economic systems. The PRC has agreed not to levy taxes on Hong Kong, and the Hong Kong dollar will remain unchanged.

Many Hong Kong residents are not convinced that this change will be in their best interests, with the result that emigration tripled between 1987 and 1991 to almost 60,000 per year. According to surveys by Kirkbride and Chan in 1988[2] and the *Ming Pao Daily* in 1990,[3] the largest group of emigrants, almost 25 percent, are in the managerial category.

There are two points of view as to how this brain drain will impact women. Those who see a shrinking economy in Hong Kong after 1997 believe that there will be fewer opportunities for women in the marketplace, according to a survey by Dolecheck and Dolecheck conducted in 1987.[4] Others, including the *Hong Kong Standard* in its 1990 poll,[5] believe that women stand to benefit from the shortage of managers caused by emigration.

WHAT WOMEN SAY

Wheeling and Dealing
When I think of Hong Kong, I think of New York City, you know— fast-paced, wheeler-dealer types. It seems like everyone is out to make a buck. Everyone is surface and there is no depth. There is no time for friendships and, if you had a friend there, I would seriously question the depth of the relationship. I remember meeting our subsidiary person in Hong Kong. He was so abrupt and full of himself. He talked fast, was "dressed to the nines" and was all business. Unlike other

countries we visited, the dinner was a mix of business and fast-paced talk. I don't think it matters much here if you are a woman. (Mountain View, California)

A Formal Affair?

There was a team of us in Hong Kong for a week of business meetings, two women and two men. We had to review numerous factory sites right over the border and have some long business discussions. The company provided us with one female and one male local sales personnel to escort us wherever we went. Naturally, the woman talked to the women and the man to the men. Our male colleagues, who were engineers, brought casual attire and one suit. The women who were in business brought one business skirt suit and two pants suits. We agreed it was a good idea to wear the skirt suit that day because a business dinner had been planned for us that night in one of Kowloon's finest restaurants. Predictably, the meeting ran overtime and we went straight to the restaurant to meet the rest of the group without time to stop at the hotel. A car pulled up with the salesman in it and then a second car pulled up with the saleswoman. She said to us two women, "You can't go out to dinner like that! You need to go back to the hotel and change into an appropriate dress." We politely declined to change as we had not brought "evening wear" on our business trip. We later asked our colleagues if they had been asked if they wanted to return to change their clothes. They had not been asked to do so. I guess you could say that this culture has some expectations for women. As businesswomen, we did not feel that we needed to adhere to their expectations, but that the standard business etiquette of wearing a suit was acceptable. (Detroit, Michigan)

Clarification Only, Please

When I was in Hong Kong with my male colleagues, we were in a meeting where there was the usual break for discussion. Communications were not very clear. I was asked a question by the supplier, but I wasn't too sure if I had understood it. I quietly leaned over to one of my male teammates in order to clarify it. He then proceeded to clarify it with our Asian counterparts and then answered for me. I later politely reminded him during a break that questions for me should be answered by me. My request was not for him to answer the question but rather to clarify to me what they had meant. I realize now that I should have asked my Asian counterpart to clarify the question for me. By asking my male col-

*league, who evidently didn't understand it any better than I did, I dimin-
ished my own position.* (Melbourne, Australia)

Punctuality Pays
*I was meeting our Hong Kong subsidiary contact for dinner. We were to
meet at 8 p.m. I was late getting out of a previous meeting. It was a very
rainy night and traffic was terrible. I arrived for dinner at 8:20. Well, my
contact was sitting at the table and had already ordered the drinks. The
first thing he said to me was how he had made his appointment despite
the rain and traffic. I got the message loud and clear. Hong Kong is a
very fast-paced city, a lot like the cities back home. Even though people
seem to be always on the run, time is important and keeping appointments and punctuality are key. (Lexington, Kentucky)*

GENERAL ETIQUETTE

From our observations and those of businesspeople we interviewed, the
points mentioned below were felt to be of particular importance for
doing business in Hong Kong. See also the general observations in Chapter 2.

> Be punctual; being on time connotes respect.

> To the Chinese, not knowing, failing to understand, or making a
  mistake can cause a loss of face, so avoid public confrontations or
  other accusatory behavior.

> If someone compliments you, the proper response is to politely deny or
  dismiss the compliment. A thank-you would be considered immodest.

> Eating food in the street, blowing your nose in public, or chewing
  gum are all considered impolite.

Body Language

People in Hong Kong use a closer personal space than their Asian sister
countries, but they do not touch each other.

> Do not point. Use your whole hand to indicate a location.

➤ Sit with your legs together and your hands in your lap. Crossing your legs may expose the bottom of your sole, which is considered impolite.

BUSINESS ETIQUETTE

Contacts

➤ As with other Chinese cultures, you have to be introduced to your target contacts before you make an appointment to see them. Do not cold call.

Greetings/Addresses

➤ Business cards are essential and should be offered along with a handshake greeting (though Chinese may bow to each other when meeting).

➤ A card with English on one side and a Chinese translation on the other is appreciated. Check to make sure whether you should use Cantonese or Mandarin. Though Cantonese is the official Chinese language, Mandarin is becoming more popular.

➤ Make a point to greet the eldest/highest-ranked members first. For formal introductions, use the person's name and title.

➤ Chinese have three names: the last (family) name is written first, followed by a generation name and then the first (given) name, though Chinese will generally follow Western style, with the surname last, when doing business.

➤ Address your Hong Kong business contacts as Mr., Mrs., or Miss. Ms. is generally not used.

➤ Use standard Western salutations when beginning letters. You need only use the person's last name, as in Dear Mr. Wong.

Appointments/Invitations

> Appointments, which may be arranged by phone or fax, are required to conduct all business.

> Because of the rapid pace of business in Hong Kong, appointments are often changed or canceled via phone or fax. Always confirm your appointments ahead of time.

> Many offices close for lunch from 12 to 2 P.M., and executives often take very long lunches. Keep this in mind when you make appointments.

> Allow extra time between meetings to get from one place to another, since traffic is very heavy and can cause delays.

Meetings/Negotiations

> For meetings you are hosting, allow half an hour of courtesy time for late arrivals.

> Introduce new ideas slowly. The Chinese are conservative and respect tradition and are unlikely to jump at new concepts or products.

> During meetings you will be served drinks, such as tea. Wait for the host to drink first.

> Hong Kong Chinese can be superstitious. Certain days are lucky, others are unlucky, as marked on Hong Kong calendars, so be aware of this when planning meetings and presentations or when signing important papers.

> Translators and consultants are readily available in Hong Kong for business travelers.

> It is easy to rent space in one of many business centers to accommodate meetings.

> Cellular phones and pagers are very common in Hong Kong and are easy for visitors to rent.

> If your company is opening an office in Hong Kong, make sure you consult a *feng shui* fortuneteller about your building location and

direction, the position of its entranceway and interior space, moving and opening dates, and any other arrangements.

ATTIRE

Hong Kong, a cosmopolitan capital, has developed a fashion consciousness that it has supported by manufacturing a flood of designer goods that are exported to other countries with European labels. Hong Kong women dress exquisitely in top designer clothes of all colors, wear a lot of fine jewelry and cosmetics, and sport the best handbags and shoes. They are very label conscious; name-brand purses and watches are status symbols. Hong Kong women spend a good portion of their disposable income on keeping up with the latest fashion trends and status styles. Shopping is a popular pastime. Most designer styles are from Europe and Japan, since Japan has many top-quality designers whose designs suit the Asian physique.

As a Western businesswoman, you will have more flexibility in what you wear than in the other three Tigers, but make sure your attire is of good quality and design. Women and men wear formal business attire year round, with skirt suits the preferred mode of dress for businesswomen. Carrying an attaché case is considered both stylish and prestigious.

GIFT ETIQUETTE

Gift-giving is not expected in Hong Kong, but if you do bring a gift it should be wrapped in red or gold paper. Red means happiness and gold means wealth. Neither blue nor white wrappings are used, since these colors signify mourning.

> ➤ If people offer you a gift, the polite response is to first decline it. If the giver persists in offering it to you, accept it with both hands and then put it away. Do not open it in front of your hosts but wait until later when you are on your own. Thank your guests in a humble manner. Gifts may be given at the end of a visit or at the end of a

dinner or meeting. If you see the gift-giver the next day, thank him or her privately. If you do not see them again, send a personal thank-you note.

➤ Giving a pair (two) of any item is considered auspicious.

➤ The Chinese consider some items unlucky, including clocks, books, hats, blankets, white, blue or black objects, and scissors or other sharp items. These should be avoided as gifts.

➤ Avoid flowers, which are suggestive of funerals.

➤ You can probably purchase almost anything in Hong Kong, which is a duty-free port. However, it is nice to bring something that can't be found there, such as native art, gourmet foods, or gift items with your company logo.

➤ Customers and clients usually exchange gifts during the Christmas holidays and Chinese New Year.

DINING ETIQUETTE

Business entertaining is key in Hong Kong. At a Chinese meal, the host will order and serve the guests throughout the meal. Everyone is expected to use chopsticks, although non-users can be accommodated. Using chopsticks (see Chapter 5, "Dining"), however, will score points with your hosts.

➤ When Hong Kong business people entertain, they will invite you out to a restaurant. You will rarely, if ever, be invited to their homes.

➤ When you arrive at a business dinner, wait until your host invites you to sit down.

➤ Wait to be seated at restaurants. If your party is small, you will most likely be seated with other diners. You do not have to socialize with them.

➤ Business discussions are usually appropriate during lunch or dinner.

➤ There is a lot of jovial conversation during Chinese meals. If you are unsure as to how to participate, a question about the food is always a good lead in. You will be served so many dishes during the meal that they will provide for continuous conversation.

➢ Other good topics for conversations include Chinese restaurants, sightseeing in Hong Kong, shopping, favorite travel destinations, and business opportunities.

➢ Wives are rarely included in business entertaining. Don't bring your husband along unless you are specifically invited to do so.

TRAVEL ADVISORY

General Information

Hong Kong includes Hong Kong Island, Kowloon Peninsula, and the New Territories, along with a number of small islands. The population, which was 6,061,400 in mid-1994, includes a large group of expatriates. Though people are continuing to emigrate, population growth rate in 1994 was 2.4 percent. Hong Kong is a Crown Colony of the United Kingdom and is scheduled to revert to China in 1997. The government is led by the Governor of Hong Kong, currently Christopher Patten.

Business Notes

Hong Kong is a free market with few tariffs or nontariff barriers. It had a 5.5% growth rate in 1994 and ranked as the eighth largest trading entity among major trading countries. Its principal trading partners are China, the United States, Japan, Germany, Singapore, and the United Kingdom. More specific information may be gained from the Hong Kong Trade Development Council, which has several offices, including:

219 East 46th Street
New York, NY 10017
Tel: (212) 838-8688

222 Kearny Street, No. 402
San Francisco, CA 94108
Tel: (415) 397-2215

HONG KONG HIGH AND LOW TEMPERATURES IN FAHRENHEIT (F) AND CENTIGRADE (C)			
	High		*Low*
JAN	64°F	18°C	55°F	13°C
FEB	63°F	17°C	55°F	13°C
MAR	66°F	19°C	61°F	16°C
APR	75°F	24°C	66°F	19°C
MAY	82°F	28°C	73°F	23°C
JUN	84°F	29°C	79°F	26°C
JUL	88°F	31°C	79°F	26°C
AUG	88°F	31°C	79°F	26°C
SEP	84°F	29°C	77°F	25°C
OCT	81°F	27°C	73°F	23°C
NOV	73°F	23°C	64°F	18°C
DEC	68°F	20°C	59°F	15°C

Currency

The unit of currency is the Hong Kong dollar (HK$), which is divided into 100 cents. There were about HK$7.80 to one U.S. dollar at the time of this printing.

You can easily obtain cash at banks and hotels, and major credit cards are accepted almost everywhere. Hong Kong is also a good place to exchange other foreign currencies. Have enough cash to cover you for essentials such as taxis, dinners (some small restaurants and stores do not take credit cards), and shopping.

Electricity/Electronics

Hong Kong electricity runs on a current of 220 volts. Presentation tapes should be converted to the PAL system.

Entry and Departure

Visitors must hold a valid passport. A visa is not required unless you are planning a stay of more than thirty days, in which case it may be extended to three months.

➤ It is better to have an outbound air ticket, since flights to and from Hong Kong are usually very full.

➤ Reconfirm your airline reservations forty-eight hours before departure. This is important—you may be bumped if you don't.

➤ The airport departure tax is HK$50.

Climate

Spring, from March to mid-May, is generally mild, with a high average humidity of about 84 percent. Summer, from late May to mid-September, is very hot, with an average humidity of about 83 percent, and is checkered with tropical rainstorms. Autumn, which begins in late September and lasts to early December, is cooler, with a lower average humidity of about 73 percent. This is sweater or jacket weather. Winter, slightly cooler than autumn, runs from mid-December to mid-March with an average humidity of 75 percent. Warmer clothes are desirable. Snow is very rare.

Public Transportation

TAXIS

➤ Taxis are numerous and reasonable. Many are color-coded. Red taxis cruise in Kowloon and Hong Kong Island, green ones in the New Territories (NT), and blue ones on Lantau Island. Have your destination written in Chinese and pay in Hong Kong dollars. Tip by rounding up to the nearest HK dollar.

TRAINS

➤ The Mass Transportation Railway (MTR) connects the Kowloon Peninsula with Hong Kong Island. It is safe, clean, and air conditioned.

➤ The Kowloon-Canton Railway (KCR.) runs from Hung Hom in Kowloon to the Chinese border. This is an interesting ride through the New Territories. You can only go as far as Sheung Shui (HK$7.50 one way) without a Chinese visa. Trains run frequently all day

BUSES

➤ Red-and-yellow minibuses can be flagged down anywhere on the island. They have about fifteen seats and are more expensive than the fixed-route buses. They will let you off almost anywhere upon request. The fare is from HK$2 to HK$7. Pay when you get off.

➤ Green and yellow maxicabs have fixed routes at fixed prices ranging from HK$1 to HK$8. Pay when you get on. The sign on the front indicates the destination.

➤ Double-decker buses cover most areas. Fares range from HK$1 to HK$30. Exact change is required. Drivers do not speak much English.

FERRIES AND HYDROFOILS

➤ The famed Star Ferry crosses from the clock tower in Kowloon to Central Hong Kong in eight minutes. Although it has recently raised its rates to HK$1.50 upper deck and HK$1.20 lower deck, it is an inexpensive and dramatic way to view Hong Kong from the water.

➤ Ferries and hydrofoils are available to Macau and the other main islands. Ask at your hotel for transportation schedules, fares, and hours.

OTHER TRANSPORTATION

➤ Trams run east-west on the north side of Hong Kong Island. These wood-paneled double-decker cars cost HK$1.20, exact change required. The Peak Tram, which runs from downtown Hong Kong straight up to Victoria Peak, offers expansive views as it traverses a very steep incline.

➤ Rickshaws are available for tourists. To locate one for a ride around the block and a few photographs, go to the Star Ferry on Hong Kong Island. Negotiate a price before agreeing to set off.

Tipping

There is some tipping in Hong Kong, but it is not nearly as pervasive as in the United States. The following guidelines should cover it.

➤ Hotels: Tipping is generally expected. As in the United States, tips are expected from the time you enter all the way up to your room.

➤ Restaurants: The restaurant automatically adds a 10 percent service charge to your bill. You are expected to leave an additional 10 percent.

➤ Taxi drivers: In general, taxi drivers don't expect tips. Small change is fine, or round up to the nearest dollar when you pay the fare. Tip HK$1–2 if the driver helped you with your luggage.

➤ Porters: Tip doormen carrying bags to registration HK$5 per bag. Tip the porter who carries your bag to your room $HK5 per bag. The hotel concierge will expect $HK10. Room service waiters receive 5–10 percent of the order if the order was good. House-keepers do not expect tips.

➤ Barbers and beauticians: These service providers expect about a 10 percent tip.

➤ Doormen, washroom attendants, and other small service providers: Tip HK$1.

Business/Banking/Shopping Hours

➤ Business hours are from 9 A.M. to 5 or 6 P.M. during the week, and from 9 A.M. to 1 P.M. on Saturdays.

➤ Banks are open during the week from 9 A.M. to 4:30 P.M. and from 9:30 A.M. to 12:30 P.M. Saturday, although this varies from branch to branch.

➤ Shops are open daily from 10 A.M. to 6 P.M. in the Central area; 10 A.M. to 9:30 p.m. in Wan Chai and Causeway Bay; and 10 A.M. to 9 P.M. in Tsim Sha Tsui.

Time to Eat

Breakfast is generally served between 6 and 7:30 A.M., lunch between 1 and 2 P.M. (though many businesspeople take long lunch hours), and dinner from 6:30 to 8 P.M.

Toilets

Toilets are marked "WC" (for water closet), like British restrooms. Most places have Western-style facilities. Toilet paper is usually provided, but bring your own for non-Western and remote facilities.

HOLIDAYS

Many holidays in Hong Kong are based on the lunar calendar, so the dates they are celebrated vary from year to year. Check those listed below that do not show a specific date to find out exactly when they are held.

National Holidays

Government offices, banks, businesses, and schools are closed on these days:

➤ *January 1*
New Year's Day

➤ *January/February*
Chinese New Year, also called Lunar New Year, is the most important holiday of the Hong Kong year. It is the time when people settle all debts, visit family and relatives, and purchase new clothes. *Lai see,* colorful money packets, are given to children and unmarried friends. Businesses close during this holiday, so be sure to check the dates before you plan your travel schedule.

➤ *March/April*
Good Friday, Easter Sunday, and the following Monday is a three-day holiday in Hong Kong.

➤ *April*
The Ching Ming Festival, which celebrates the beginning of spring, is traditionally one of two occasions during the year when families visit and sweep the gravesites of their ancestors. The other, Chung Yeung, is in October.

➤ *June*
The Birthday of Queen Elizabeth is usually held on a Saturday in June. The following Monday is generally also a national holiday.

➤ *June*
Dragon Boat Festival, because it falls on the fifth day of the fifth moon, is also called Tuen Ng ("Double Fifth"). Colorful festivities commemorate the death of a young poet, Ch'u Yuan, who drowned himself in the third century B.C. to protest government corruption. Competing crews in long, slim boats plow through the waterways to the beating of drums as an enormous crowd cheers them on.

➤ *Last Monday in August*
Liberation Day commemorates Hong Kong's liberation from Japanese troops in 1945.

➤ *September*
During the Mid-Autumn Festival, families meet for lavish dinners and eat mooncakes while they gaze at the full autumn moon.

➤ *October/November*
The Chung Yeung Festival, held on the ninth day of the ninth month is one of two during the year (see Ching Ming Festival, above) when families visit and sweep the gravesites of their ancestors.

➤ *December 25*
Christmas Day.

➤ *December 26*
Boxing Day.

Other Holidays and Festivals

➤ *Last Day of Chinese New Year*
Yuen Siu, sometimes called Chinese Valentine's Day, is celebrated by festooning homes and streets with brightly colored lanterns.

➤ *April*
Tin Hau, a festival for the goddess of the sea, is celebrated by brilliantly decorated fishing junks that converge at seaside temples to pay her colorful homage.

➤ *May*
Buddha's Birthday is observed by bathing statues of the great sage.

➤ *July*
Lu Pan, the patron saint of builders and craftsmen, is honored on his birthday by lavish banquets.

➤ *August*
The Hungry Ghosts Festival is celebrated by laying food out on doorsteps and burning offerings to appease the hunger of ghosts who have been released on a short reprieve from hell.

➤ *August*
The Seven Sisters or Maidens Festival is a celebration for lovers and a time when single women pray for good husbands.

➤ *September*
Confucius' birthday is commemorated with special observances held at the Confucian temples.

RECOMMENDED HOTELS, RESTAURANTS

The list below includes places we think would be comfortable for women and, in the case of restaurants, suitable for entertaining business clients. We have rated our hotel recommendations from $$ to $$$$, with $$$$ being the most expensive (e.g., over HK$1,500 per night).

Kowloon Hotels

➤ *Regent Hotel ($$$$)*
Salisbury Road
Tsim Sha Tsui, Kowloon
Tel: 2721-1211
Fax: 2739-4546
Pluses:
• Excellent view of the harbor from its famed bar and outdoor whirlpools
• Outdoor pool
• Airport pick-up

Minuses:
- No in-room modem hook up
- No 24-hour news cable channel
- No non-smoking rooms
- No in-room checkout

➢ *Hyatt Regency Hong Kong ($$$)*
67 Nathan Road
Tsim Sha Tsui, Kowloon
Tel: 2311-1234
Fax: 2739-8701
Plus:
- Regency Club floors, with special amenities for members

Minuses:
- No pool or fitness center
- No courtesy airport transportation
- No garage

➢ *Peninsula ($$$)*
Salisbury Road
Tsim Sha Tsui, Kowloon
Tel: 2366-6251
Fax: 2722-4170
Pluses:
- Elegant older Hong Kong hotel
- Convenient location next to Kowloon harbor

Minuses:
- No in-room checkout
- No garage

➢ *Kowloon Shangri-La Hong Kong ($$$$)*
64 Mody Road
Tsim Sha Tsui East, Kowloon
Tel: 2721-2111
Fax: 2723-8686
Pluses:
- Waterfront location
- Excellent health club
- Elegant white-marble motif

➢ *Hong Kong Renaissance ($$$)*
8 Peking Road
Tsim Sha Tsui, Kowloon
Tel: 2375-3311
Fax: 2375-6611
Pluses:
• Laptop PC rentals
• Louis XVI decor
Minus:
• Business Center closed on Sundays

Kowloon Restaurants

➢ *Capriccio*
Hong Kong Renaissance, 2nd Floor
8 Peking Road
Tsim Sha Tsui, Kowloon
Tel: 2311-3311, ext. 2260
• Northern Italian cuisine.
• Reservations required. Formal attire.

➢ *Gaddi's*
Peninsula
Salisbury Road
Tsim Sha Tsui, Kowloon
Tel: 2366-6251, ext. 3989
• French Supper Club.
• Reservations required. Formal attire.

➢ *Shang Palace*
Kowloon Shangri-La Hong Kong
64 Mody Road
Tsim Sha Tsui East, Kowloon
Tel: 2721-2111
• Cantonese dining.
• Reservations required. Formal attire.

➢ *The Delicatessen Corner*
Holiday Inn Golden Mile
50 Nathan Road

Tsim Sha Tsui, Kowloon
Tel: 2369-3111, ext. 147 or 250
- No reservations required. Casual dress. This deli, open until midnight, is a comfortable place for single women to dine alone.

Hong Kong Island Hotels

➢ *Grand Hyatt Hong Kong ($$$$)*
1 Harbour Road
Wan Chai, Hong Kong
Tel: 2588-1234
Fax: 2802-0677
Plus:
- Extensive health club with outdoor swimming pool
Minuses:
- No in-room checkout
- No courtesy airport transportation

➢ *Mandarin Oriental ($$$$)*
5 Connaught Road Central
Hong Kong
Tel: 2522-0111
Fax: 2810-6190
Plus:
- Convenient location
Minuses:
- No courtesy airport transportation
- No in-room checkout

➢ *J. W. Marriott Hotel Hong Kong ($$$$)*
Pacific Place, 88 Queensway
Hong Kong
Tel: 2810-8366
Fax: 2845-0737
Minuses:
- No in-room checkout
- No garage

➢ *Island Shangri-La Hong Kong ($$$)*
Pacific Place, Supreme Court Road, Central

Hong Kong
Tel: 2877-3838
Fax: 2521-8742

Hong Kong Island Restaurants

➤ **Excelsior Grill**
Excelsior Hong Kong, 3rd Floor
281 Gloucester Road
Causeway Bay, Hong Kong
Tel: 2837-6783 or 2894-8888
  • Reservations required. Formal attire. This local favorite features an inexpensive salad bar during the lunch hour and more formal dinners, including dishes such as chateaubriand. It has a piano bar.

➤ **Parc 27**
Park Lane, 27th Floor
310 Gloucester Road
Causeway Bay, Hong Kong
Tel: 2890-3355, ext. 344
  • Reservations required. Formal attire. This is an upscale French restaurant with a panoramic view of the harbor and Victoria Park.

➤ **Aberdeen Floating Restaurants**
  • There are three floating restaurants in Aberdeen Harbour that can be reached by motor ferry. They feature local Chinese and seafood cuisine with fanfare and flourish for the tourist trade. The food is not particularly great, but most visitors go for the experience.

WHAT TO SEE AND DO

➤ **Star Ferry**
We recommend this eight-minute harbor ferry ride between Kowloon and Hong Kong Island. It offers a great view of both areas for next to nothing.

➤ *Drinks at the Regent Hotel*

A must-do for the first time visitor, this is Hong Kong's number one sightseeing attraction. The view from the bar is the most spectacular on the island.

➤ *Peak Tram Ride*

This provides a terrific view of Hong Kong on a clear day. The tram takes about eight minutes to climb the steep slope from downtown Hong Kong Island to the top of Victoria Peak, offering stunning views along the way. Open from 6 A.M. to midnight.

➤ *Cultural Shows*

The Hong Kong Tourist Association (HKTA) sponsors free weekly cultural shows at their center, which is within walking distance of most Kowloon hotels. Excerpts from Peking operas, puppet shows, acrobatics, martial arts, etc., are highly recommended.

➤ *Middle Kingdom*

This miniature landscaped replica of the Chinese Middle Kingdom re-creates 5,000 years of Chinese history. It is located next to Ocean Park, on the south side of Hong Kong Island.

➤ *Sung Dynasty Village*

This historic re-creation in northern Kowloon features authentic-looking buildings from the Sung Dynasty a thousand years ago with actors in period costumes, a Chinese wedding, acrobatic shows, and Kung Fu demonstrations.

➤ *Tiger Balm Gardens (Aw Boon Haw Gardens)*

This peculiar garden on Hong Kong Island offers eight acres of bizarre foliage, outlandish cement structures and creatures, and tableaux depicting often gruesome moral lessons.

➤ *Aberdeen*

This is a former fishing village on the southwest side of Hong Kong Island. Catch a local water taxi out to one of the floating restaurants, such as the Jumbo or TaiPak. Natives consider the food touristy, but the ornate environments are a must-see. The ride itself is worthwhile as you will wend your way through many interesting boat residences along the route.

➤ *Cat Street Center*
This district, a former hang-out for sailors on shore leave, housed prostitutes and opium dens and was generally patronized by toughs. Located on western Hong Kong Island, it has since been renovated into a shopping area with interesting curio shops and small eateries.

➤ *Fung Ping Shan Museum*
Chinese arts are displayed in this small, Hong Kong University–run museum on Hong Kong Island.

➤ *Happy Valley Racecourse*
Packed with gamblers, this famous track on Hong Kong Island is a great place to amble around and people watch.

➤ *Ladder Street*
Climb this long, cement "staircase" 200 feet up the hill on western Hong Kong Island and check out its multitude of street sellers and small shops along the way.

➤ *Other Attractions*
There are a number of theaters, concerts halls, stadiums, and centers for the performing arts. Hong Kong has a philharmonic orchestra, dance company, and repertory theater groups. There are also many museums housing collections of Chinese artifacts.

➤ *Hong Kong Ferries*
These water boats and hydrofoils offer a variety of day trips and island excursions to Macau, the New Territories, and Cheung Chau, Lamma, Lantau, and Peng Chau islands. Some islands have good swimming beaches, others offer great hikes, seafood restaurants, and stalls selling items such as traditional herbs, incense, and candles. Go to Macao for gambling casinos (take a photo I.D. with you) and delicious Portuguese cuisine and wines.

Temples

Foreigners generally find the Taoist temples, with their legions of colorful god and goddess figures on the rooftops, the most interesting to visit. Inside, you will find locals burning incense to the gods, tossing divination sticks to seek the answer to a question, or pulling a fortune paper to learn their destiny. Hong Kong also has a number of Buddhist and Confucian temples. At the Buddhist temples, which have venerated statues of the Buddha, people worship by praying, lighting incense, and bringing offerings of food for the Buddha's nourishment.

TEMPLE ETIQUETTE

➤ Shoes may be worn around temple courtyards but must be removed before you enter any of the roofed buildings.

➤ When you pass through the temple gate or any of the inner doorways, be sure to step over, never on, the raised threshold.

➤ Don't take photographs inside Buddhist temples unless you have obtained permission to do so.

WORTH VISITING

➤ *Man Mo Temple*
A Taoist temple dedicated to the gods of war and literature, Man Mo is located on Hollywood Road in western Hong Kong.

➤ *Po Lin Monastery*
On Lantau Island, this temple complex features a magnificent 80-foot-high statue of Buddha.

Nightlife

Hong Kong has its share of "hot" pubs and discos. Ask your associates and hotel concierge what is hot and what is not while you are there. Eating out and gambling in Macao are popular choices for visitors, but you can find just about anything you want in Hong Kong, from karaoke clubs to movie theaters and dance spots.

For information on night spots and other activities, check the two Hong Kong publications, *Hong Kong This Week, Hong Kong Diary,* and *The Official Hong Kong Guide,* available at most newsstands and hotels.

SHOPPING

A favorite local pastime, shopping is also the main Hong Kong attraction for visitors. In fact, visitors are said to spend almost three-quarters of their time in Hong Kong shopping. Women travelers we interviewed recommend that you bring a large expandable suitcase, a list of things you need for the next year, a list of gifts to buy for your family and friends—and lots of cash. Most businesspeople say that they either lay over in Hong Kong for a breather after visiting other parts of Asia or stay for a weekend of shopping. Hong Kong does have many great bargains in jewelry, clothing, luggage, and so forth if you know your brands. There are a lot of imitations out, however, so be very careful where you shop. Most high-fashion goods can be purchased at reasonable prices. Silk is a very good buy and readily available. Electronics are available, but pricing depends on consumer demand. Everything is negotiable. You can expect to negotiate a 30 percent discount on most items and up to 50 percent on others. Keep in mind, however, that shopkeepers can be quite aggressive. Products sold in fine stores and department stores have fixed prices.

Shopping Tips

➤ Bargaining is expected, but don't start bargaining for an item unless you plan to buy it or the shopkeeper will become angry. Do not bargain at department stores or boutiques, since prices are fixed.

➤ If you are going to bargain, know how much up front you are going to pay for an item, and then you can walk away if you don't get the deal. Many times it is the "walking away" that makes or breaks the sale. If you walk away and the shopkeeper agrees to your final price, you must be ready to pay up. If you walk away and the shop doesn't meet your price, you must be able to live without the item.

➤ If you plan to shop and bargain, it is best not to wear good clothes but go in rags (casual wear), if possible. Definitely leave all your jewelry in the hotel safe.

➤ If you are bargaining for a high-ticket item, look for any flaws and position yourself as saving the shopkeepers by taking it off their hands.

➤ Don't be chatty. If you are pursuing an item, act businesslike and disinterested.

➤ Bargain alone, if you can. If you are with someone, have them say negative things about the price and comment that the store down the street had it at a cheaper price. Watch your theatricals, however. Salespeople can size up your intentions fairly easily.

➤ Bargaining in Hong Kong takes time. If you don't have the time, it may not be worth opening up negotiations. Instead, pay the price and move on to other things in your schedule.

➤ For some items, like electronic goods, bring newspaper ads from home and take them to the shops to make sure you are really getting a better price in Hong Kong.

➤ There are some department stores, called Chinese Friendship stores, that feature only goods from China.

➤ Before you make a credit card purchase, inquire if the store imposes a surcharge for using a credit card.

➤ Make sure that any warranty matches your purchase (check the serial number) and that it applies worldwide.

➤ Check to make sure all the attachments are included with the product you are purchasing.

➤ If you are buying gold pieces, check to make sure they are stamped with their weight.

➤ Ask your hosts or the hotel concierge for a reputable place to buy pearls, since imitations are common. The same goes for jade, which is popular and reasonably priced.

➤ Eyeglasses are reasonably priced in Hong Kong and can be ready for pick up within a day or two. There is a large selection of fashionable frames and a cursory eye examination is provided. Nevertheless, to be perfectly sure, bring your prescription from home.

Silk

Silk is a great buy in Hong Kong. Check the item you want to make sure the stitching is sound and that it is not stained or torn. Shop the local

USEFUL CANTONESE PHRASES

English	Pronunciation
How are you?	Nay hoh mah
Good morning	Joe sun
Goodbye	Joy wui
Please (invitation)	Cheng
Thank you	Dor chay
Excuse me	Mm-goy
I am sorry	Doi mm-jew
Yes	High
No	Mm-high
I understand	Ngor ming
I don't understand	Ngor mm-ming
How much?	Gay dor cheen

Precise romanization of Cantonese is problematic, so this chart presents only approximate pronunciations. The extensive use of tones to distinguish words from each other in any case makes pronunciations very difficult to learn from phrase books. English is generally understood in Hong Kong.

marketplaces such as the Night Market and Nathan Street, where there are numerous small silk exporters who are willing to bargain on just about everything, including today's outbound shipment. The quality of the silk you receive for the price may be debatable. It is fairly easy to find low grades of silk at inexpensive prices. The higher grades you might find may be just as pricey or even more expensive than what you can obtain from discounters at home. We have had the most success by either visiting the markets and picking up pieces from broken sets (blouses, pants, skirts) or visiting an exporter shop that is selling off extra or slightly flawed jackets or blouses.

Women's Tailors

There is some debate about whether it is still worth having clothes made in Hong Kong; tailors seem to be more expensive than they were in the past. It may, however, be worth considering if you have an outrageously priced designer outfit in mind or are hard to fit.

Jewelry

There are numerous jewelry stores in Hong Kong, and we will not even venture to suggest where to shop. The best advice we can give is for you to know your prices and get an outside appraisal if the piece you want is expensive. When making major purchases, make sure the HKTA mark is displayed, and get a certificate detailing the purchase you have made as well as a detailed gemological appraisal of both set and unset stones. For watches, get the manufacturer's guarantee, the serial number, and the warranty of the watch you purchase. Much of the gold in Hong Kong is 18K, but can run up to 24K.

Antiques

Hollywood Road is the prime area for antique and memorabilia shops. It is located on Hong Kong Island in the western district within walking distance of the Sheung Wan MRT stop. Go with a word of caution from the experts that many of the items are indeed fakes. If you are interested in real antiques, it is well worth your time to find a reputable dealer.

Markets

Hong Kong seems to have a surplus of markets. There are fruit and vegetable markets, jade markets, women's markets, men's markets, and general merchandise markets. The marketplaces consist of stalls and shops on the streets or in the shopping malls. Prices are negotiable; this is where you can test your bargaining mettle.

➤ *Peddler Building*
Located at 12 Peddler Street on Hong Kong Island, this market contains enough outlet-type stores and restaurants to occupy you for a full day of discount shopping. Some of the stores are not necessarily discount shops, but there are plenty for comparison shopping.

➤ *Stanley Market*
Also known as Stanley Village, this extensive outdoor bazaar is located on the south side of Hong Kong Island. It has declined in popularity over the years (so we are told by those who know). Items tend to be jumbled together in makeshift stalls for bargain appeal, but the goods are often as expensive as those in the stores. The bus

ride from Central is interesting and you can pick up touristy items there like T-shirts, bathing suits, and souvenir trinkets.

➤ *Nathan Avenue*
This whole street on Kowloon is a market, with hawkers touting everything from clothes and electronics to luggage. For more interesting, more negotiable bargains, try walking up a few flights of stairs to the small hole-in-the-wall shops along the sides of the avenue.

➤ *Jade Market*
The jade market is an outdoor market in the Yau Ma Tei district on Kowloon that is packed with stalls selling jade items. It is open from 10 A.M. to 3:30 P.M. daily. Make sure the jade license is posted, but don't accept the stall's assurance that it is jade. Most may be fake or a cheap version of a white jade dyed green to look more valuable. Bargain down to about 50 percent of the advertised price. Since the market is small and word gets around quickly, try not to insult a stall owner or no one will serve you. If you cannot determine the difference between real and imitation jade, or don't want to take a chance, it may be wiser to look in certified jewelry stores.

➤ *Temple Street Night Market*
Outdoor stalls located outside temples in Kowloon's Yau Ma Tei district and filled to capacity with all sorts of merchandise operate from 8 to 11 P.M. nightly. As you wander around the myriad goods for sale, you may see amateurs trying their vocal skills at Chinese opera gatherings, or orange sellers spinning fruit at lightning speed to remove the peel in one long unbroken spiral.

7 | Taiwan

When you go to Taiwan on business, I suggest that you be very sensitive to the ownership of the company, know whether it is family-owned or not and the ages of the people you deal with. If they are older, they will be more Japanese influenced and more biased against women in business, more doubtful of your capability. You will easily fit in with younger people and there will be no question about your capabilities, since they often have been educated in the West and have a stronger U.S. influence. . . . If you're of the older generation, I suggest you think more about establishing your credibility through rituals and protocol. (New Haven, Connecticut)

Taiwan is a Confucian society with all that that implies about women being subservient to men. But while the people of Taiwan are still greatly influenced by their Confucian upbringing, the younger generation has been exposed to the U.S. and other Western cultures and has been quick to adopt a more westernized view—Taiwan is way ahead of Korea, for example, in terms of westernizing its culture. Yet a 1991 study of female university students in Taiwan shows them to be more self-effacing than males in Taiwan or U.S. females.[1] Women in Taiwan tend to adhere to the Chinese cultural value of modesty and to the qualities and gender-role stereotypes of women as being socially responsible and congenial but relatively incompetent in comparison with men.

A 1992 study by Michael Tang of 500 women managers in the Taipei metropolitan area indicated that women are growing in self-confidence and are discarding traditional stereotypes.[2] Still, Tang pointed out that "they believe that they have fewer occupational opportunities than men, particularly in regard to compensation, promotion, organizational environment, and dual-career marriages or relationships. They attribute this lack of opportunity to structural barriers rather than to lack of ability." The study indicated that women tend to listen better and to be more responsive to people's needs. Women, it said, try to develop a consensus, to gather and integrate alternative points of view, and to build teams. This, the study said, does not always work to their advantage since male managers tend to be more assertive and independent. Yet the same study indicated that women who adopt a more aggressive, independent style are viewed negatively in male-dominated companies—a perfect double bind!

Tang's survey found that women in Taiwan are generally thought of as unassertive, lacking in self confidence and leadership skills, and not tough enough to handle the business environment. Taiwan women would rather settle for a comfortable niche in a company than make the necessary sacrifices to reach a top position. Women in business are encouraged to become managerial or public relations assistants or to work in customer service. Thus, while men in Taiwan pursue the managerial positions, women end up as specialists, a role that blocks them from attaining the top jobs.

This situation, however, is not as severe in Taiwan as it is in Korea or Japan. In Taiwan, 46 percent of all women are reported to have received higher educations, including graduate degrees—placing it first in Asia and twelfth in the world—according to UNESCO figures. This reflects the prevailing desire for equal opportunity for all, as well as the government's desire to utilize its human resources to the fullest. In fact, women with graduate degrees are being found in management positions in ever-increasing numbers in Taiwan. And they are vocal critics of discriminatory corporate policies. Women fuel Taiwan's labor-intensive garment industry. They also provide the "manpower" for computer industries, such as the manufacture of silicon chips.

A study on wage discrimination in Taiwan[3] found that females received lower earnings than males for the same experience, firm size, and marital status. Although the law requires equal pay for men and women, Business International reported in 1992[4] that management positions are occupied for the most part by men, who earn about 30 to 40 percent more than women. Although over 41 percent of all professionals in 1990 were women, only 9 percent were managers. Further, working hours for females and minors are more restricted than those for males. Women need special permission to work between the hours of 10 P.M. and 6 A.M. Overtime is restricted to twenty-four hours a month for females, compared to forty-six hours a month for males.

Since women are still the primary child caretakers on Taiwan, almost half of the respondents in the Tang study indicated that their jobs interfered with their marriages and relationships. Rising divorce rates in Taiwan and an increasing number of women (43 percent) who are remaining unmarried suggest a bleak picture for dual-role marriages in Taiwan. Single women complain that they are often passed over for promotion because of management fears that they will marry and quit. Although it is illegal to dismiss women when they marry, the law is not strictly enforced and the practice is still fairly common. A labor shortage due to a rapidly expanding economy and a low birth rate (only 1.1 percent in 1990) is pushing more firms to accept married women who wish to resume work.

Maternity leave and other benefits for women are quite liberal in Taiwan. But these concessions may also impact advancement opportunities. Married women who take advantage of companies that offer flexible working hours, childcare, and maternity-leave benefits complain that they are being passed over when it comes to partnership offers, higher salaries, promotions, and desirable assignments. Most of the women in the Tang study agreed that women must be exceptional to succeed in business in Taiwan.

This overview of women in Taiwan is not meant to suggest that Western businesswomen will necessarily face the same barriers. In fact, Western women are likely to be treated more deferentially and to be more readily accepted for their credentials and skills.

DOING BUSINESS IN TAIWAN

Taiwan formed its own government in 1949 after the Chinese Nationalist Party under Chiang Kai-shek lost a civil war in China to the Communist party. Chiang fled to Formosa, which was renamed Taiwan. Since then, the island nation has experienced rapid economic growth. Taiwan, along with the other three Asian Tigers, is classified as a newly industrialized economy (NIE) and is now one of the most dynamic export-oriented economies in Asia. Unlike Hong Kong and the United States, which are free-market economies, much of Taiwan's commerce is regulated by government controls. Education, transportation, health, and agricultural development are subsidized by the government. There are also many government-owned monopolies, such as the bus and railroad facilities, banking, telecommunications, sugar, tobacco, and liquor. Private industry, however, is flourishing, and business is gradually being liberalized and deregulated.

To the visitor, Taiwan appears to be homogeneously Chinese, very densely populated, and under constant construction. Unlike Hong Kong's capitalistic high-rise style and Singapore's squeaky-clean environment, Taiwan seems an endless industrial and high-tech site. Like the mainland Chinese, the people of Taiwan have a Confucian underpinning and a strong work ethic. Following the Confucian teaching to be strict with yourself but benevolent to others, people are polite and gracious.

People in Taiwan have, however, been strongly influenced by the West, which has diluted their traditional values over time. What is good for the self and family now takes precedence over what is good for the country. Some of these changes may become evident to you through observing the companies with which you work. Though some retain the traditional belief that the owner is all-powerful and the employees are part of the family network, others seem to be moving away from tightly controlled family reigns toward offering employee equity and promotion based on achievement.

Women report that working in Taiwan is relatively easy. The more westernized a company is, the more women it employs and the higher their positions will be. Most women comment that they experience a difference in attitude between the older and younger generations in Taiwan. For the most part, the older generation is traditional and strongly influenced by Japanese values that date back to Japan's occupation of Taiwan between 1895 and 1945. Many older people will be fluent in Japanese. In general, if you are working with older people in Taiwan, you may find you need to establish your credibility more than if you are working with the younger generation, many of whom are quite accustomed to working with Western women.

WHAT WOMEN SAY

A Host for Her!
I was visiting a rural town in Taiwan as a company guest. Our company group of six was male, except for me. There was only one hotel in town, with a restaurant and bar. Staying in the hotel room was undesirable as it was pretty small, dismal, unsanitary, and without TV. We had no choice but to hang out in the bar or restaurant. So we met downstairs in the bar. When we walked in, our Taiwan contact, a man who had been there before, ordered a table for six. He then added, "five women and one man." I wasn't too sure what he meant. We were ushered to our table and were promptly followed by five female hostesses and one male "host" for me. This was our company for the evening. As soon as we sat down, the women were all over the men and the man was all over me. At that point I stood up and politely said that I had to leave. Thankfully, my male colleagues also stood up and said that they also had to leave. As we had made a very strong point as a team, our Taiwan contact apologized and sent the hostesses away. The rest of the evening went fine. (Syracuse, New York)

Lunch—Give Me a Break!
I was in Taiwan alone on this trip doing supplier updates. I'm very good about preplanning, sending agendas, and confirming appointments. At a meeting in the supplier's Taiwan office, I was met by the executives, who held a very short meeting with me. When it was time for lunch, I was introduced to a group of women who had been selected to accompany me at mealtime. None of the male executives were included in this group. I politely responded that I had a luncheon appointment elsewhere, but thanked them profusely for their generous offer. I said this because I felt that while they were trying to be gracious to me, as the sole woman it would be to my disadvantage to dine with these women; it would emphasize my difference from the rest of the team. At the same time I did not want to insult my host by saying that it was not appropriate. I rather opted to state that I had plans elsewhere, hoping to make my point subtly. It worked. The next day we all dined together. (Boise, Idaho)

Defer, Defer, Defer

On my first trip to Taiwan with a male team, I concluded that Western men can hurt your credibility. Now I work with them to help me. For example, on this trip a Taiwan contact asked one of my male colleagues a question he was not qualified to answer. He made something up just so that he could answer the question. What was worse, I was sitting there with the answer. He obviously answered because the eye contact was made with him and his ego needs were too strong to defer. Men need to defer to the team member who knows the answer to the question. In this case it was me. After the meeting we had a review in our group. We talked about how to handle these kinds of situations. My male colleague admitted that he wasn't sure what to do and was feeling a little bit "on the spot" because they seemed to focus on him for an answer. We developed a strategy on how to defer to each other so that we appeared stronger as a team. In Western companies we are all leaders in our own right and it can be very confusing to a hierarchical society as to who is on top and who is on the bottom. Many times all participants in the Western group are of equal rank. Our Asian counterparts often assume that the oldest male is the leader as it is in their culture, unless they are otherwise advised. (Vancouver, Washington)

Break Time

My male colleagues and I attend numerous meetings with a company in Taiwan. People in Taiwan also travel extensively to the U.S. to visit us. It is an all-male group except for me. At our first formal meeting in Taiwan, everyone treated me very graciously. Later, several secretaries joined the meeting. During the break, they ran over to me and started a conversation. This happened during every break. At lunch I was seated next to them as well. They had nothing in common with me and did not know the business at hand. I eventually mentioned to one of my Taiwan contacts that I would feel more comfortable sitting and chatting with my counterparts. I did say that I appreciated their hospitality and graciousness in trying to provide me with female companions. He looked surprised, so I added with a smile that even if they are men, I am accustomed to this. (Austin, Texas)

GENERAL ETIQUETTE

From our observations and those of businesspeople we interviewed, the points mentioned below were felt to be of particular importance for doing business in Taiwan. Refer also to the more general discussion in Chapter 2.

➤ Punctuality is vital; it indicates respect and consideration of people's busy schedules.

➤ Avoid loud, aggressive behavior.

Body Language

➤ Do not touch anyone. In particular, do not touch children on their heads.

➤ Women may cross their legs when they sit down, but men should keep their feet flat on the floor. Always point the soles of your shoes away from others, since the feet are considered to be dirty and unsuitable for touching either objects or people.

➤ Do not eat or drink in the street.

➤ Waving a hand in front of your face usually means no.

➤ To point, use your whole hand rather than your index finger.

➤ You will be jostled a lot in large crowds and in lines. When this happens, don't get angry, just push and shove along with everyone else.

BUSINESS ETIQUETTE

Contacts

➤ You may need either a letter of introduction or a personal introduction from a mutual friend or a bank to get an appointment—or even a reply—from businesspeople you want to meet.

➤ Build your relationship before you start to do business, since Chinese prefer to deal with individuals with whom they have a relationship.

Greetings/Addresses

➤ Chinese usually have three names: a one-syllable family name followed by a generation name and a first name. Some businesspeople, however, have adopted the Western style of putting their family name last. This can be confusing! If you are unsure about the family name, ask.

➤ When you address people, always try to use their titles and family names. Mr., Mrs., and Miss may be used, but it is best to stick to titles, especially in formal situations. Since you know that Mr. Wu is a doctor, you would address him as Dr. Wu.

➤ Many Chinese who deal with foreigners use a Western first name for business; for example, Dr. Wu calls himself Edward Wu. Do not, however, address your Taiwan business contacts by their first names unless they ask you to do so.

➤ When introduced, follow your host's lead. Handshakes are acceptable, though Chinese will often make a slight bow.

➤ Always allow your host to enter a room, elevator, or vehicle first.

Appointments/Invitations

➤ Business appointments are necessary and must be scheduled in advance.

➤ For social events, the initial invitation is often made by phone, then confirmed by mail.

Meetings/Negotiations

➤ When you select a negotiating team, choose people who have a good knowledge of your overall company operations, regardless of their rank.

➤ "Yes" can mean either "yes" or merely "I understand what you are saying." "Maybe" usually means "no." Flatly disagreeing is impolite.

➤ Instead of boasting about your company's successes, let your company's written material speak for itself. It is polite to downplay your achievements and possessions—even when you are talking about your family.

➤ Don't expect to return home with a contract or completed negotiations. Concluding a business deal takes time.

➤ Taiwan firms, out of polite consideration, may provide Western women with the companionship of female employees of possibly lower rank. The best way to handle this is to be polite but continue your business discussions with your appropriate counterparts.

ATTIRE

When it comes to doing business in Taiwan, it is best to dress conservatively. Suits are preferred and may also be worn to dinner. Be particularly conscious of color and design; it is better to be too conservative than too fashionable. For example, a male friend confided that many Western businesswomen wear red "power suits." In Taiwan, he said, neither red nor gold are worn in business but rather for festivities. A woman, he advised, would be taken more seriously if she wore conservative colors like navy blue and gray. If you are in Taiwan on business to celebrate something, however, a bit of red adds a nice festive touch.

Most business is conducted in Taipei, the capital and largest city in Taiwan. People are very fashion oriented. Much of the clothing imported by Western nations is manufactured in Taiwan, so most international businesspeople will be very well dressed in top-of-the-line business attire. Other cities in Taiwan, however, are very conservative and not as fashionable. You might, in fact, be surprised by their lack of style. Consequently, a conservative suit will serve you well either in Taipei or in the countryside. Lower heeled shoes are recommended to help you maneuver around the potholes in the roads and cracks in the sidewalks. Taipei is always under construction, so you will often find yourself in the midst of rubble and rocks when trying to grab a taxi or get to a restaurant. Purses and bags are status symbols. If you choose to carry one, make sure it is a good brand.

You can generally identify executive women in Taiwan by their suits and outfits, often purchased during shopping vacations to Hong Kong (considered the Asian fashion Mecca, much as Paris is the place to buy clothes in the West). European designs, which can be readily purchased at good prices in Hong Kong, are favored. Working-class women who do not have much disposable income will most likely be wearing locally manufactured clothing and shoes.

Some women change into dinner dresses for dinner, but this is not necessary. We recommend that if you are wearing a suit for a business meeting, wear it to dinner as well. Skirts and jackets and dresses with jackets are more favored in the daytime business environment than pants suits. Avoid black or white clothing; these colors are worn at funerals.

In the cool, humid winter months, wool suits, jackets, and dresses are best since wool soaks up moisture while keeping you warm. For the hot, humid months, linens and cottons are more comfortable. Bring a raincoat for the frequent showers (business hotels generally offer them for use by their guests).

GIFT ETIQUETTE

Gift-giving does take place in Chinese culture and in Taiwan, though it is not as prevalent as in Korea or Japan. Gifts are usually only token items.

➢ Bring a small gift for a person you are meeting for the first time or for your dinner host.

➢ Protocol demands that gifts be wrapped. However, save the wrapping until you enter the country as your packages may be unwrapped by customs officials. Business wrapping paper is fine. Red and gold papers are considered rich and festive.

➢ Chinese often exchange money in lieu of gifts. In the business world, however, stick to customary Western business gifts.

➢ Always present or receive a gift (or any other object) with both hands to show respect.

➢ In Chinese culture, it is polite to first refuse an offered gift. You are expected to persist until the recipient agrees to accept it. If your gift is still refused after the third offer, quietly put it away.

➤ You will not always receive a gift in return. If you are proffered a gift, a little modesty can go a long way. You may also try a little of the "No, I couldn't possibly" yourself before being persuaded to accept it.

➤ When you visit a company, particularly around New Year's, bring a small gift such as a box of sweets that can be shared.

➤ The recipient of the gift never opens it in the presence of the person who gave it, but politely puts it aside to be opened later.

➤ Gifts with your corporate logo, framed pictures, and framed Chinese characters representing fortuitous or wise sayings are well received as gifts, as are fine pens and pencil sets. Gifts of liquor such as wines or brandies, especially from your local area, are usually acceptable, unless you know that your hosts do not drink alcohol.

➤ Appropriate gifts for company openings include flower stands (round, wreath-like arrangements of real or artificial flowers atop a wooden frame). A ribbon banner across the front displays Chinese characters wishing luck, money, success, and so forth. These can be purchased at Taipei florists. You will see many of them on the streets in front of new shops and restaurants.

➤ Do not give clocks and watches, since the pronunciation of the word "clock" is similar to the word for "death." Items that cut, such as letter openers or scissors, are considered to be bad luck since they imply the severing of a relationship. Handkerchiefs are not given as gifts since they can signify the departure of someone or something.

DINING ETIQUETTE

Business entertaining is generally done at good Chinese restaurants and can be very expensive.

➤ If an eatery is crowded, you may be seated at a table with other diners. You are not expected to talk to them.

➤ Do not discuss business while you are eating unless your Chinese host brings up the subject.

➤ Good topics for conversation include Chinese food, art, the culture of Taiwan, and families.

➤ If you host a banquet, arrange to pay the bill before the meal begins, or excuse yourself to pay discreetly out of sight of the diners just before the meal ends.

➤ After someone treats you to a dinner, reciprocate with a dinner of equivalent value.

TRAVEL ADVISORY

General Information

Taiwan, with a population of 21,170,832 (1994) and a growth rate of about 0.96% (1992), is nearly three times the size of Connecticut. Taiwan has a one-party presidential regime, with opposition political parties. The chief of state is President Lee Teng-hui, who was elected in 1990. The next elections are scheduled for 1996. There is no diplomatic representation for Taiwan, which is officially called the ROC (Republic of China) by its government. Unofficial commercial and cultural relations with the United States are maintained through the private Taipei Economic and Cultural Office (TECO), previously called the Coordination Council for North American Affairs (CCNAA).

Business Notes

Taiwan is an export-driven, capitalist economy with government guidance of investment and trade, as well as partial ownership of some large banks and industrial firms. Taiwan has, however, joined the trend toward liberalization now sweeping many Asian nations. The fourteenth largest trading nation in the world, with a GDP growth rate of about 6.4% (1994), its principal trading partners are the United States, Japan, Hong Kong, and Germany. For more information, contact:

Far East Trade Service (FETS)
555 Montgomery Street, Suite 603

San Francisco, CA 94111
Tel: (415) 788-4304

Additional FETS offices are in New York, Chicago, and Miami.

Currency

Taiwan's unit of currency is the New Taiwan dollar (NT$), which is divided into 100 cents. There were about NT$25 to one U.S. dollar at the time of this printing.

You can easily obtain cash at banks and hotels. Major credit cards are accepted in hotels and tourist-oriented restaurants and stores.

Electricity/Electronics

Taiwan electricity runs on a current of 110 volts. The VHS system is used for VCRs, in case you bring a video presentation tape.

Entry and Departure

Visitors must possess a valid passport and a visa, regularly covering stays of up to two months. Businesspeople may also need a letter of guarantee from their company with a statement that they are traveling on business for the company, information about the nature of the business and whom they are seeing, and a return airline ticket. Contact the Taipei Economic and Cultural Office (TECO) at:

4201 Wisconsin Avenue NW
Washington, D.C. 20016
Tel: (202) 895-1800

Branches are also located in other major cities.

➤ Have enough cash to cover essentials such as taxis, shopping, and food items.

➤ You will have to pay an airport departure tax when you leave Taiwan. Check with your hotel for the current rate.

	High		Low	
	TAIWAN HIGH AND LOW TEMPERATURES IN FAHRENHEIT (F) AND CENTIGRADE (C)			
JAN	66°F	19°C	54°F	12°C
FEB	66°F	19°C	54°F	12°C
MAR	72°F	22°C	57°F	14°C
APR	77°F	25°C	64°F	18°C
MAY	84°F	29°C	70°F	21°C
JUN	88°F	31°C	73°F	23°C
JUL	93°F	34°C	77°F	25°C
AUG	91°F	33°C	77°F	25°C
SEP	88°F	31°C	73°F	23°C
OCT	82°F	28°C	68°F	20°C
NOV	75°F	24°C	63°F	17°C
DEC	70°F	21°C	57°F	14°C

Climate

Taiwan has a tropical climate with two seasons: a hot season from May to October and a cool season from December through March. It rains frequently during the spring and in December. Between July and October are damaging typhoons and rainstorms with very strong winds. The most pleasant times to travel to Taiwan are March through May and September through November, when there is less rainfall. The humidity, which can be debilitating, hovers around 80 percent on up.

Public Transportation

TAXIS

➤ Taxis, probably the easiest way to get around, are inexpensive and easy to find. Paradoxically, puzzled-looking foreigners seem particularly able to attract them.

➤ Pick up taxis from hotels, restaurants, and offices. Be sure to keep your hotel and destination address written in Chinese to show the driver; most taxi drivers speak very little English. Double the time you think it would take to get where you are going, since traffic is very congested. If your hosts have not provided you with transportation, you may want to ask them to help you secure a taxi.

➤ Women traveling alone in Taiwan should be especially cautious when obtaining transportation. If you hail a taxi, check to make sure there is no one in the back seat before you get in.

TRAINS

➤ Taiwan has an excellent train system that is ideal for intercity travel. The express class is more expensive than the highway buses, but well worth the extra money.

➤ The Taipei train station is downtown, near the tourist hotels. Trains are very heavily used, so try to reserve your seat several days before your trip. Once you have your ticket, look on the back to find your carriage and seat numbers, as well as the platform number, which may be included.

BUSES

➤ There are two kinds of buses, regular and air-conditioned. Tour buses, which travel to scenic destinations, are very comfortable. They must, however, be reserved in advance.

Tipping

The government and the hotel industry discourage tipping. However, there are times, such as when someone provides an extra service, when a tip will be appreciated.

➤ Hotels: A 10 percent service charge is usually included in the bill, so tipping is not necessary. A small tip to the bellhop for carrying your bag, however, won't be refused.

➤ Restaurants: A 10 percent service charge is usually included. If not, leave a 10 percent tip.

➤ Taxi drivers: Tips are not expected unless the driver helps with your luggage. The customary tip for this is NT$30–$50.

➤ Porters: Tip NT$20 per piece of luggage.

➤ Barbers and beauticians: 10 percent of the bill.

Business/Banking/Shopping Hours

➤ Business hours during the week are from 9 A.M. to 12 P.M. and 1:30 P.M. to 5:30 P.M. Saturday business hours are from 9 A.M. to 12 P.M.

➤ Banks are open during the week from 9 A.M. to 3:30 P.M., and from 9 A.M. to 12 P.M. Saturday.

➤ Shops are open daily (including Sundays) from 10 A.M. to 10 P.M.

Time to Eat

Breakfast is generally served between 7 and 8 A.M., lunch between noon and 2 P.M. (the usual office lunch hour is between noon and 1 P.M.), and dinner from 6 to 8 P.M.

Toilets

There are Western-style toilets available in good hotels and most commercial buildings. However, you may occasionally encounter an Asian-style squat toilet, a rectangular porcelain fixture in the floor with a raised "cup" at the front. Watch your hem and bring tissues with you.

HOLIDAYS

Many holidays in Taiwan are based on the lunar calendar, so the dates they are celebrated vary from year to year. Check those listed below that do not show a specific date to find out exactly when they are being held.

National Holidays

Government offices, banks, businesses, and schools are closed on these days. All national holidays that fall on a Sunday are observed on the following Monday.

➤ *January 1–2*
New Year's Day is also Founding of the Republic of China (Taiwan) Day and celebrates the inauguration of Dr. Sun Yat-sen as first Provisional President of the New Republic of China (Taiwan) with parades, dragons, and lion dances.

➤ *January/February*
Chinese Lunar New Year is celebrated with feasts, parades, and lion and dragon dances. It starts on the first day of the first moon. The holiday lasts three days, but many people take the entire week off from work. Most offices are closed, so do not plan to do business in Taiwan at this time.

➤ *March 29*
Youth Day.

➤ *April 5 (April 4 in leap years)*
Tomb-Sweeping Day/President Chiang Kai-shek Day is a day when people visit family gravesites to sweep and clean the graves of their ancestors.

➤ *June*
The Dragon Boat Festival on the fifth day of the fifth lunar month commemorates the suicide-by-drowning of the ancient poet Ch'u Yuan, who was protesting a corrupt government. Dragon boat races are held on Taipei's Tamsui River.

➤ *August or September*
The Mid-Autumn Festival or Mooncake Festival, on the fifteenth day of the eighth lunar month, marks the autumn harvest with moonwatching and eating special mooncakes.

➤ *September 28*
The Birthday of Confucius is celebrated by ancient dances performed to ritual music and other festivities at the Confucian temples.

➤ *October 10*
National Day (Double Ten Day) commemorates the founding of the Republic of China (Taiwan) in 1911 with a huge parade in front of the Presidential Building in Taipei.

➤ *October 25*
On Taiwan Retrocession Day there are athletic events and lion and

dragon dances to celebrate the end of Japanese control and the return of Taiwan from Japanese to Chinese rule after the war.

➤ *October 31*
Chiang Kai-shek's Birthday.

➤ *November 12*
Sun Yat-sen's Birthday.

➤ *December 25*
Constitution Day/Christmas Day.

Other Holidays and Festivals

➤ *February/March*
The Lantern Festival, held fifteen days after the Chinese New Year, is observed by decorating temples, squares, and other public areas with colorful lanterns. Children have their own special lanterns, which they often create themselves.

➤ *February*
Kuan Yin's Birthday, on the nineteenth day of the second lunar month, celebrates the birth of the god/goddess of mercy.

➤ *April/May*
Ma Tsu's Birthday commemorates the birth of the goddess of the sea with temple celebrations.

➤ *April 4*
Women's and Children's Day.

➤ *May*
Buddha Bathing Festival honors the great sage by parading Buddha images through the streets and sprinkling them with water to cleanse and purify them.

➤ *August*
Ghost Month is celebrated in the seventh lunar month. Most Chinese do not travel at this time, when ancestral ghosts are believed to be wandering about.

RECOMMENDED HOTELS, RESTAURANTS

The list below includes places we think would be comfortable for women and, in the case of restaurants, suitable for entertaining business clients. We have rated our hotel recommendations from $$ to $$$$, with $$$$ being the most expensive (e.g., over NT$5,300 per night).

➤ *Grand Hyatt ($$$$)*
2 Sungshou Road
Taipei
Tel: (02) 720-1234
Fax: (02) 720-1111
Pluses:
• Regency Club floor, with amenities for members
• Service is among the best in Taipei
Minuses:
• No in-room checkout
• No hairdresser

➤ *Regent Taipei ($$$$)*
41 Chungshan North Road
Section 2, Taipei
Tel: (02) 523-8000
Fax: (02) 523-2828
Plus:
• Health club with extensive facilities, rooftop pool

➤ *Grand Hotel ($$)*
1 Chungshan North Road
Section 4, Taipei
Tel: (02) 596-5565
Fax: (02) 594-8243
Pluses:
• Convention facilities
• Health club with pool, tennis courts, bowling alley
Minuses:
• No computer rentals
• Away from city center

➤ *Sherwood Taipei ($$$$)*
111 Minsheng East Road
Section 3, Taipei
Tel: (02) 718-1188
Fax: (02) 713-0707
Pluses:
- Located downtown
- Shuttle service

➤ *Lai Lai Sheraton ($$$)*
12 Chunghsiao East Road
Section 1, Taipei
Tel: (02) 321-5511
Fax: (02) 394-4240
Pluses:
- Downtown location
- Shuttle service

➤ *Howard Plaza ($$$)*
160 Jenai Road
Section 3, Taipei
Tel: (02) 700-2323
Fax: (02) 700-0729
Pluses:
- Downtown location
- Shuttle service

Restaurants

Taiwan is an excellent place to try all types of Chinese food. There are a number of fine restaurants around Taipei offering both Chinese and international cuisine. You can usually get excellent recommendations from your hotel concierge, from the free weekly local information magazines found in the hotel lobby, or through your Taiwan business contacts. Since most business travelers are in town for business meetings or conventions and their time is very limited, we have provided a starter list of several good Chinese restaurants located in popular Taipei hotels.

CANTONESE

➤ *Golden Dragon*
Grand Hotel, 2nd Floor
Tel: (02) 596-5565, ext. 1112 or 1229
- Serves some of the best Cantonese cuisine found in Taipei.

➤ *Canton Garden*
Grand Hyatt, 2nd Floor
Tel: (02) 720-1234, ext. 5513
- Authentic Chinese cuisine with a twist of creativity. Private dining rooms are available.

➤ *Man Han Palace*
Asia World Hotel, 3rd Floor
Tel: (02) 715-0077, ext 308
- Cantonese cuisine in a Chinese palace environment.

HUNAN

➤ *Tien Hsiang Lo*
Ritz Taipei Hotel, Basement 1
Tel: (02) 597-1234, ext. 240 or 200

➤ *Hunan Garden*
Lai Lai Sheraton Hotel
Tel: (02) 321-5511, ext. 8016/17

SHANGHAI

➤ *Shanghai Court*
Grand Hyatt, 1st Floor
Tel: (02) 720-1234, ext. 3241
- Traditional Shanghai cuisine with French service.

➤ *Yangtze River*
Howard Plaza, 3rd Floor
Tel: (02) 700-2323, ext. 2300 or 2301

SZECHWAN

➤ *Chinese Dining Room*
Grand Hotel, 2nd Floor
Tel: (02) 596-5965, ext. 1216 or 1229
  • A choice of dishes from Szechwan and Shanghai cuisines.

➤ *Szechwan Restaurant*
Ambassador Hotel, 12th Floor
Tel: (02) 551-1111, ext. 174 or 175

TAIWANESE

➤ *Formosa*
Howard Plaza, Basement 1
Tel: (02) 700-2323, ext. 2300 or 2301
  • Most Taiwanese cooking is found in local restaurants around
    town. The Formosa offers you the opportunity to try Taiwanese
    food in the environment of a good hotel.

➤ *Happy Garden*
Lai Lai Sheraton Hotel, 2nd Floor
Tel: (02) 321-5511, ext. 8011 or 8012

WHAT TO SEE AND DO

➤ *Chiang Kai-shek Memorial Hall*
This great, white hall honors Chiang Kai-shek with a mammoth
statue and displays his achievements. Surrounded by a park, it dom-
inates its Aikuo East Road location. Open 9–5 daily.

➤ *Presidential Square*
This is the center of Taiwan's government offices, including the
imposing Presidential Building and Ministry of National Defense.
Find it at Chungching South Road northwest of Memorial Hall

➤ *National Palace Museum*
Ranked as one of the top four museums in the world, this treasure
house of thirty centuries of Chinese art from Beijing's Forbidden

City is a definite must see. This magnificent collection of Chinese art, with 650,000 pieces, was rescued and moved to Taiwan beginning in 1933. The displays, which rotate every three months, are labeled in Chinese and English. The tea house on the roof provides views of the surrounding hills and pots of aromatic Chinese teas. Take a taxi to its location some twenty minutes north of Taipei. Open 9–5 daily.

➤ *Martyrs' Shrine*
This memorial commemorates all those who died fighting for China. It was designed to resemble Beijing's Hall of Supreme Harmony. Located on Peian Road northeast of the Grand Hotel, it is open daily from 9 to 5.

➤ *National Museum of History*
This museum displays Chinese art dating from 2000 B.C. It is located at the Botanical Gardens near the National Art and Science halls.

➤ *Wulai Aboriginal Village*
Costumed, tattooed aboriginal Atayal Taiwanese perform tribal dances. Tips are expected for performances and photos. The shops feature handwoven goods made locally by tribal women who demonstrate their techniques. Located about fourteen miles south of Taipei, there is a narrow-gauge rail car from the village to a waterfall and an aerial cable car to Dreamland Forest Recreational Park.

Temples

TEMPLE ETIQUETTE

➤ Shoes may be worn around temple courtyards, but must be removed before you enter any of the roofed buildings.

➤ When you pass through the temple gate or any of the inner doorways, be sure to step over, never on, the raised threshold.

➤ When you're in a Buddhist temple, don't take photographs unless you have obtained permission.

USEFUL MANDARIN CHINESE PHRASES

English	Mandarin	Pronunciation
Hello	Ni hao	Knee how
How are you?	Ni hao ma?	Knee how mah
Goodnight	Wan'an	Wahn ahn
Goodbye	Tsai-chien	Dsigh jyan
Please	Ch'ing	Cheeng
Thank you	Hsieh-hsieh	Shay shay
You're welcome	Pu k'o-ch'i	Bu ke-chi
I am sorry	Tui-pu-ch'i	Day-bu-chi
Excuse me	Lao-chia	La-oh-jah
I don't know	Wo pu chih-tao	Waw bu jer-dow
I don't understand	Wo pu tung	Waw bu dawng
How much?	Tuo shao ch'ien?	Daw-sha-oh chew-an

Chinese dialects like Mandarin and Cantonese make extensive use of tones to distinguish words from each othe. This makes pronunciations very difficult to learn from phrase books. You should not have much trouble with English in Taiwan as long as you stay in the touristed areas. Chinese is written using several thousand pictographic characters. The "spellings" of Chinese words here are given in the Wade-Giles system of romanization.

WORTH VISITING

➤ *Lungshan Temple*
Dedicated to Kuan Yin, the goddess of mercy, this is one of the most popular temples in Taipei. The oldest and most colorful Buddhist temple in the city, it is usually packed with people of all ages. Find it on Kuangchou Street, west of the Botanical Gardens.

➤ *Pao An Temple*
This Taoist temple on Chiuchuan Street west of Chungshan North Road has dragons decorating its roof and columns. Red-robed monks officiate inside. Directly across the street is a Confucian temple that has dances and music on September 28 to honor Confucius' birthday.

SHOPPING

Taiwan has a lot of shopping, but few real bargains still exist. Some good prices, however, are still to be found in toys, clothing, sporting goods, and local jewelry. Hardware items may also be good bargains. Fake brand-name goods abound, so beware of counterfeits. In the shops, salespeople will often follow you around closely as you shop and perhaps offer you a beverage to soften you up for a sale. You may accept the drink; there is no need to oblige them by buying something.

Shopping Tips

➤ Bargaining is common in shops where items are not marked.

➤ Bargains in clothing and housewares are easier to find during the weeks before Chinese New Year when shopkeepers need cash to pay off old debts before year end. Food, however, is more expensive.

Markets

The night markets are good places to find bargains and haggle over prices. If you don't speak Chinese, carry a pen and paper so you can make written offers and counteroffers.

➤ **Snake Alley Night Market (*Huahsi Street*)**
This is one of the most exotic night markets in Asia and is a popular spot for most tourists, since it is very close to Lungshan Temple. The street got its name from the many shopkeepers who keep live snakes in cages. When there is enough of a crowd for a show, the shopkeeper hangs a live snake on a wire, then cuts it open down its entire length with a knife. The bile and blood are mixed with strong liquor and offered to onlookers for about NT$100 a shot. These shows have been losing popularity, due to increased sensitivity to wildlife issues, but you might be lucky enough to spot one. For the most part, Snake Alley has become simply a large night market for tourists.

Handicrafts

➤ *Taiwan Handicraft Promotion Center/Chinese Handicraft Mart*
Located at 1 Hsuchow Road near the East Gate, this bazaar is loaded with brass, lacquerware, jade, marble, and bamboo items at reasonable prices.

➤ *China Pottery Arts Company*
This is the place to go for ceramics. You'll find it on Nanking East Road.

8 | *Singapore*

When I was in Singapore in 1990, I attended then-President Lee Kuan Yew's yearly State of the Union speech. As I recall, he put up a chart on the Singapore birthrate. His goal was to have a more educated population bred in Singapore. To an American it sounded absurd. In essence, he was trying to control the population. He offered tax incentives for educated couples to have three or four children and cash incentives for uneducated women to be sterilized. I feel that what Lee was trying to accomplish went directly against the Chinese culture and mentality. In the Chinese culture, the man typically marries below his station and the woman above. Lee wanted to break this tradition in exchange for a "better" population. He had no interest in the love aspect of relationships. (Philadelphia, Pennsylvania)

Confucian ethics still have a strong foothold in Singapore, as in the other three Asian Tigers. But the government also plays an important role in shaping Singaporean life. As the anecdote above relates, the government has particularly strong feelings about a woman's social role as a mother and even seeks to control which women become mothers. Thirty percent of Singapore's female college graduates remain unmarried and childless into their thirties. There is also the phenomenon of "hypergamy," the tendency for local women to desire richer and more educated husbands. For their part, Singapore men still prefer wives who are controllable and thus prefer to marry women who are less educated than they are. Because the Chinese are reproducing at a much lower rate than the

Malays and Indians in Singapore, the government has instituted match-making services to facilitate marriage among the educated Chinese, who form almost 76 percent of the population.

In 1983, women made up 35 percent of the total employed population. By 1991 this had grown to 51 percent. Due to a shortage of labor in Singapore caused by the nation's rapid economic development following its separation from Malaysia in 1965, and a desire to reduce the number of foreign workers in the market, the government started a campaign to lure married women into the working world. It initiated child care, flexible work schedules, and a public campaign to change society's attitudes toward working women.

Prejudicial employer attitudes and unfair company practices were seen as the main barriers to women's advancement. A 1989 survey by Audrey Chan[1] found that female college graduates had to search for jobs longer than their male counterparts, received fewer job offers, and were less satisfied than male graduates with their starting salaries.

Married women in Singapore are considered unsuitable for jobs that require frequent travel, managerial positions supervising men, and supervisory positions at "macho" locations such as construction sites, shipyards, and manufacturing plants. Employers doubt that mothers will be able to work the necessary hours and question whether their customers respect and trust women in managerial positions. Female managers have reported hostility from clients, colleagues, and subordinates in the office. Inadequate support from men and, surprisingly, from other female colleagues, left many feeling alone and lacking in authority. Furthermore, because of their upbringing and social pressure, female managers in Singapore may have difficulty exercising their power. According to the Chan study, women are considered shortsighted in setting career goals, reluctant to take on major managerial and decision-making responsibilities, and deficient in the political skills necessary to advance.

According to a study by Chan and Lee in 1994,[2] most female managers in Singapore are concentrated in personnel, administration, consumer affairs, and public relations, and most are in lower- and middle-management positions and in support functions rather than line positions.

Singapore women we interviewed for this book claimed that they do not see many females in top executive positions in Singapore. Traditional views about women are still apparent in the classified sections of local newspapers, where employers openly state their search for female employees in advertisements. An example: "Looking for secretary between 22–27. Must be pretty, educated, with warm qualities and be able to serve coffee and socialize with excitement." Female managers in Singapore also have difficulty developing the business networks necessary to enhance their careers. Much business is done on the golf course and in private clubs, which are still generally male preserves.

With all these overt and *de facto* barriers, many Singapore women trying to juggle a family and career—both of which they are expected to give top priority—become discouraged by the extra effort needed to reach the top. Those women who are willing to make the effort face unfavorable attitudes toward their assertiveness and a higher burnout rate than men. They not only risk remaining unmarried or seeing their marriage end in divorce, but they must also accept that they will have less time to spend with their families. (Furthermore, behind every successful woman are probably two others in subservient positions—a maid, and a mother who lives nearby.) A recent study examining conflicts faced by married professional women in business shows how women are suffering increasing levels of work-family conflict, anxiety about their children's welfare, and generally decreased levels of satisfaction with their daily lives.[3]

Of course, women are latecomers to corporate life in Singapore, so how successful they will be in reaching top management positions remains to be seen. It is important to remember that this discussion is merely a snapshot of the current situation for local businesswomen in Singapore. For Western businesswomen the situation is different. Because they are foreigners, they receive more formal and respectful attention.

DOING BUSINESS IN SINGAPORE

The first-time visitor to Singapore may be surprised at its cultural diversity. The population is mostly Chinese, but there are also large Malay and Indian populations. And after other Asian countries, this city-state will seem particularly clean and westernized. While it is true that Singapore is an English-speaking country, the predominant culture is Chinese. The government and business communities are influenced by Confucian values that emphasize a strong work ethic, which many feel has contributed to Singapore's success. The government exerts tight control;

people are expected to vote and put money in savings. There is a very high literacy rate. Everything is done for the good of the country and the family.

Possibly the most striking feature of the Singaporeans for Westerners is a seeming lack of individual opinions. Very few people speak out openly, since individual views must also be subordinated to the common good. You should therefore avoid questioning your hosts about sensitive topics such as government policies. You are unlikely to get an answer and will only make your host feel uncomfortable.

Singaporeans tend to be somewhat materialistic, and most visitors will be amazed at the number of shopping and eating places on the island. Status is also important, with all its trappings. With the current large demand for labor, Singaporeans, unlike most Asians, tend to job hop and show little allegiance to their companies.

Most Western women say they find it easy to conduct business in Singapore. Compared to other Asian countries, women can be found in more levels of business and are usually well educated. As one business-women observed, however, there are a lot of Western firms in Singapore and a lot of joint ventures. These firms tend to offer more opportunities to women and minorities (Malays) than the Chinese-owned companies, which tend to be more traditional. Another woman noted that most of the business establishments are male oriented. "When we have business lunches at the local business restaurants, I see very few women at the tables and in the business clubs. However, I am accepted because I am a Western woman, so I feel more comfortable about doing business in Singapore than I do in Japan or Korea."

You may find it difficult to enter the inner circles, since they are very tight. On one of our first visits to Singapore, we dined with a close friend of a friend who gave us a tour of the area and some local insight. When we went to conduct business at a subsidiary of our firm the next day, we were relieved at how easy it was to work with our counterparts. There were plenty of woman in middle management positions with whom to interface. We did notice, however, that they seemed somewhat remote, even though we worked for the same company. During one conversation, my counterparts asked us how we had spent our weekend. We mentioned that we had dined with a friend. As it turned out, they knew him quite well. After that we were accepted fully. We had broken the first barrier to establishing relationships in Singapore.

Singapore is cited as being the safest country among the Four Tigers, with relatively little overt sexual harassment. Although the country appears to be very Western, it is wise to remember that you are still dealing with a Chinese-based society.

WHAT WOMEN SAY

In-house Training
I was doing a training program in Singapore, and I made an agreement with my male co-trainer to let me take the majority of questions and not to interject unless it was critical. I felt it was important to make sure that this group viewed both the man and the woman equally. I knew that I would need to assert my authority a little more in the beginning. Well, that worked out very well. At first, the men looked to him and the women to me, but eventually they accepted that we were both credible presenters. I think it is important to understand that, as a woman, you may be viewed as having less credibility than a male colleague, even when your credentials are equal. I think it is important to work with your male colleagues to help you establish your credibility. You may need to work harder, but once you have successfully established your credibility, you will never lose it. (Boston, Massachusetts)

Management Training
As an expatriate manager of an all-women group in Singapore, the biggest difference I see is that women defer to the corporate personnel, Caucasians, and men. It is part of their class system. So I found it a challenge to get them to push back as we do in Western society. I felt that I needed to help them learn how to assert themselves, even if it wasn't part of their culture; otherwise they just get stomped on. When you go into a meeting in Singapore, you will find that the women will automatically defer to the men. Interestingly enough, many assumed that I would also defer in the same way. As a Western manager, I felt that I needed to assert myself and also organize my team based on their credentials and not their gender. We actually developed into quite a strong team. (Singapore)

The Presentation
As a European woman who is gregarious, I found myself being watched

in amazement by the Singaporean women. I was there to give a presenta-
tion on our new policies. Instead of listening to me, I found that they
were just watching me. I use a lot of gestures and intonation. I speak
loudly and laugh a lot. I think this all was pretty unusual coming from a
woman. They just watched me as I asserted myself in my usual style. I
hear they talked about me for a long time afterward. Women in Singa-
pore are very soft spoken; they use very few gestures and are not openly
expressive. I guess my style, while comfortable for me, may have been
overwhelming, so now I try to remember to tone it down a little bit,
because I want them to pay attention to my presentations and not my
movements. (Cork, Ireland)

Dress for Success?
Singapore is a very hot and humid place. Our team had arranged to meet
at the hotel and have a pre-meeting before our meetings the next day.
The pre-meeting ensures that we leave and arrive at the meeting together.
One of the engineers stated that he preferred to stay in another hotel,
which was his regular place. He decided that since he was at a different
hotel and was familiar with Singapore, he would take a cab and meet us
at the office. Well, he was late for the meeting and arrived wearing
shorts. I was very surprised and annoyed by his actions. I walked him
outside and suggested that he could join our meeting when he was
appropriately dressed. I reminded him that we were a team and that the
actions of one individual could reflect poorly on the others. Furthermore,
I reiterated that Singapore business protocol, despite the heat, included
the wearing of long pants for men. He went back and changed. (New
York, New York)

Singapore Smiles
We were at a team meeting in Singapore. We had not met our Singapore
team members previously except through electronic mail. There was an
equal balance of women and men from both sides. What was confusing
was that the U.S. contingency would present a point and the Singapore-
ans would agree—no debates, no discussion. They smiled at us all the
time, but then later on they would act differently and blatantly against
the agreement. I think that Singaporeans tend to agree with people in an
effort not to be confrontational and cause conflict. I also think they are
caught between agreeing with the company (who pays their bills), acting
as an individual (driven by their Chinese background), and acting for the

benefit of the country (driven by the Singaporean government). There seems to be this undercurrent that even though you are in agreement on what is best for the firm, if the individual or the country's needs differ, they will be prioritized. Now I try to sit down with my colleagues after our meetings to try to find out if they really agree with the points made or not. I think you need to do that in a smaller setting and ask their opinions and feelings on a lot of the issues before moving ahead with a decision. (Vancouver, Washington)

General Etiquette

From our observations and those of businesspeople we interviewed, the points mentioned below were felt to be of particular importance for doing business in Singapore. You should also review Chapter 2 for general business practices.

➤ The government in Singapore uses Mandarin Chinese, although English is widely used as the business language.

➤ Elderly people are accorded great respect.

➤ Compliments are appreciated but are usually modestly denied.

➤ Public displays of affection are frowned upon.

Body Language

➤ The head is considered to be the home of the soul and therefore should not be touched.

➤ The feet are the lowest part of the body and are considered too dirty to be used for touching objects.

➤ Be careful when crossing your legs; the sole of the foot should never be pointed at or even inadvertently shown to other people.

➤ When you're standing and talking to someone, do not put your hands on your hips since this signifies anger.

➤ Do not hit your fist into your other cupped hand; this is an obscene gesture.

➤ Beckon someone by extending your hand, palm down, and fluttering your fingers.

➤ Cover your mouth with your hand when you yawn.

➤ It is considered rude to blow your nose or clear your throat in public.

➤ Be aware of and observe all the local laws and fines for littering, spitting, etc.

➤ Since most Malays are Muslims, be aware of specific behaviors that would offend them. For instance, only use your right hand to shake hands or hand things to people, since the left hand is considered unclean. Do not share food and do not allow the serving cutlery to touch your plate at communal dinners. Make it a point to wash up both before and after dinner.

BUSINESS ETIQUETTE

Greetings/Addresses

➤ Singapore is hierarchical, like other Chinese cultures, so titles are important. When meeting your Singaporean contacts, the higher-ranked and more elder members should be addressed first.

➤ Western-style written salutations for business correspondence are the most common. For example: "Dear Mr. Wang."

➤ As in all Asian cultures, it is important to establish your credibility. If possible, have someone from your home office or someone in Singapore introduce you, emphasizing your credentials.

➤ Bring a lot of business cards. Present your card with your name and title in English. It is not necessary to have it translated into Mandarin on the back unless you are dealing with a Chinese company.

➤ Men and women usually greet each other with a handshake. Muslim Malays may bring their right hand back to their chest after they shake hands.

Appointments/Invitations

➤ Set up appointments in advance.

➤ Westerners are expected to be on time, so be punctual. If you can't avoid being late, phone ahead. You can usually get to appointments on time, since the business center is compact.

Meetings/Negotiations

➤ Be punctual for meetings.

➤ Singaporeans try to avoid conflict. Remember that nods of the head or murmurs of agreement may only signify that you have been heard and understood, not that your listener agrees with you. After the big meetings, you will need to clarify all agreements in smaller settings to be sure that everyone is in agreement.

➤ Keep your voice well modulated and minimize your hand and body gestures.

➤ If someone laughs or smiles at what seems like an inappropriate moment, don't be surprised or angry; smiling is often used to mask real feelings.

➤ Before you leave home, arrange appointments by fax. Business-people in Singapore travel frequently and are often out of the office.

➤ Westerners are often deferred to in Singapore. It does not mean that you will be agreed with, or that your judgment call is necessarily correct. You must always verify your counterparts' thoughts and positions.

ATTIRE

Though Westerners often associate tropical environments with vacation-and-leisure attire, Singapore, like the other three Tigers, expects conserv-ative business garb. The look for both men and women, however, is more casual than in other Asian capitals.

Singapore is hot and humid all year around. You may need to develop a hot-climate wardrobe if you plan to travel there frequently. Wear natural fabrics that breathe, such as cotton. Many women incorporate linen and washable silk pieces into their business wardrobe, which helps them deal with the heat. In business, you will see jacketless men wearing short-sleeved shirts and an occasional tie. Businesswomen wear stockings and tailored linen and silk dresses, with many opting for lightweight linen and silk pants suits.

Like Hong Kong, Singapore is very fashionable. While women do not dress as boldly as they do in Hong Kong, they nevertheless value their designer brands. Because Singapore is a duty-free port, you can find a wide variety of quality designer clothes at reasonable prices. For business, wear a sleeved blouse and skirt or a pants suit. Short sleeves are acceptable, but avoid wearing sleeveless blouses. For casual wear, your best bet is a skirt or slacks.

GIFT ETIQUETTE

> Gifts are generally not given until a business relationship has been established. Have one ready in your briefcase, however, just in case you receive one.

> Singapore is corruption free, so be careful not to give any gift that could be construed as a bribe.

> If someone gives you a gift, reciprocate with a gift of about equal value or a dinner invitation.

> Gifts are never opened when they are received or in the presence of the person who gave them.

> When you wrap your gifts, be aware of the significance of color for the different cultures in Singapore. Malays associate white paper with funerals, while yellow is reserved for royalty. The Chinese associate white, black, and blue wrapping paper with funerals. Red and gold are good for wrapping gifts for Chinese Singaporeans, who consider them celebratory colors. The Indian culture uses green, red, or yellow paper for gifts.

> Sweets, fruits, cakes in reusable tins, and crafts from your home

region are considered appropriate gifts. Items with your company logo, such as pens, neckties, and paperweights, are also appreciated.

➤ Do not give clocks or watches as gifts, since Chinese cultures associate them with death.

➤ Letter openers and scissors should also be avoided, since these are associated in Chinese cultures with severing a relationship.

Dining Etiquette

➤ Business lunches are more often preferred to business dinners.

➤ If you receive an invitation to lunch or dinner, accept if at all possible.

➤ If you are invited to dinner, it will almost always be at a restaurant. You will rarely be invited to a Singaporean home.

➤ Spouses are more often able to attend dinners and other functions in Singapore than in other Asian countries if the function or dinner is social and business will not be discussed.

➤ If you are invited out to dinner, do not expect to have drinks and appetizers beforehand. Let the host order all the dishes.

➤ If you invite others to a dinner, try to have an even number of people at the table to ensure good fortune.

➤ If a restaurant is crowded, ask someone if you can share their table; at medium-class restaurants, the waiter will ask for you.

➤ If you have any dietary restrictions, tell your host discreetly before the meal.

➤ At a lunch or dinner, you will usually find four to six serving dishes in the middle of the table. You will be given your own bowl of rice.

➤ Wait until your host begins eating and invites you to start.

➤ When you serve yourself from a communal dish, don't let the serving spoon touch your plate, since anything that touches someone's plate is considered to taint it.

➤ Don't offer your leftover food to anyone, not even your spouse or children.

➤ Singapore Chinese eat with chopsticks, while Malays and Indians eat with spoons or their right hands.

➤ If you're given a spoon and fork, hold the spoon in your right hand and the fork in your left.

➤ Indian food is sometimes served on a banana leaf.

➤ When you eat *satay* (grilled meat on skewers), use the skewers to spear and eat the rice cakes and garnishes.

➤ If you're given steamed, filled buns (*baozi*), eat them with your chopsticks. Don't pick them up with your fingers.

➤ If someone offers you a drink, accept it with both hands, your left hand supporting your right and your right hand grasping the glass. Offer drinks the same way.

➤ Before and after a meal, always make a point of going to the washroom to clean up.

➤ To get a waiter's attention, simply raise your hand, palm down, and flutter your fingers in a beckoning gesture.

➤ It is considered impolite to clear your throat or blow your nose at the table.

➤ Good topics of conversation at a meal are economic growth, multicultural traditions, local cuisines and restaurants, favorite travel destinations, and your host's business success.

➤ Subjects to avoid at table include discussions of a personal nature, local politics, racial friction, and religion. People will not discuss the government or government regulations, so don't ask about them.

TRAVEL ADVISORY

General Information

Singapore, formally called the Republic of Singapore, is a small city-state off the southern tip of Malaysia that can be reached via a 1.1-km-long causeway. It comprises the main island of Singapore and some fifty-seven scattered islets. Lion City, as it is called, is about 3.5 times the size of Washington, D.C., with a population of 2,873,800 in 1994 and a growth rate of about 1.2%. The current chief of state is President Ong Teng Cheong, who was elected in 1993, though past Prime Minister Lee Kuan Yew, who headed Singapore for many years, still has a lot of influence.

Business Notes

Singapore is a thriving open-entrepreneurial economy with strong service and manufacturing sectors and solid international trading links. The GDP growth rate of 10.1% in 1994 was among the highest in Asia. Singapore's top trading partners are the United States, Japan, and Malaysia. For more information, contact:

> Singapore Trade Development Board
> 55 East 59th Street, No. 21-B
> New York, New York 10022
> Tel: (212) 421-2207

Branches are located in major U.S. cities.

Currency

The unit of currency is the Singapore dollar (S$), which is divided into 100 cents. There were about S$1.39 to one U.S. dollar as of this printing. Cash can be acquired at banks and hotels. Major credit cards can be used at all but the smallest shops, and travelers checks can be exchanged at banks and hotels.

SINGAPORE HIGH AND LOW TEMPERATURES IN FAHRENHEIT (F) AND CENTIGRADE (C)				
	High		*Low*	
JAN	82°F	28°C	77°F	25°C
FEB	88°F	31°C	81°F	27°C
MAR	88°F	31°C	81°F	27°C
APR	88°F	31°C	81°F	27°C
MAY	88°F	31°C	81°F	27°C
JUN	88°F	31°C	81°F	27°C
JUL	88°F	31°C	81°F	27°C
AUG	88°F	31°C	81°F	27°C
SEP	88°F	31°C	81°F	27°C
OCT	88°F	31°C	81°F	27°C
NOV	88°F	31°C	81°F	27°C
DEC	82°F	28°C	77°F	25°C

Electricity/Electronics

Singapore electricity runs on a current of 220 volts. Presentation tapes should be converted to the PAL system.

Entry and Departure

Visitors must have a passport and onward or return ticket. A visa is not required for tourist and business stays of up to two weeks, extendable to a maximum of three months. For more information, contact:

> Embassy of the Republic of Singapore
> Washington, D.C. 20008
> Tel: (202) 537-3100

➤ The airport departure tax is S$15.

Special Regulations

The Singapore government enforces many ordinances that apply to local residents and visitors alike. Littering, jaywalking, possession of chewing gum, smoking, spitting, leaving toilets unflushed, graffiti, and possession of certain drugs are considered serious offenses. Punishment ranges from fines to physical punishment, prison, and death.

Climate

Singapore is very close to the equator and has a tropical climate. Relative humidity can exceed 90 percent at night, so the temperature will seem much hotter than it actually is. The wettest months are from November to January. Storms are frequent and downpours can be heavy, so bring an umbrella.

Public Transportation

TAXIS

➤ Taxis abound in Singapore and are the most popular mode of transportation for business visitors. They are inexpensive. You can catch one at a taxi stand or hail one in the street. Some surcharges apply when you are traveling into restricted zones (business districts and shopping areas).

TRAINS

➤ The MRT (Mass Rapid Transit) subway is inexpensive, clean, and safe. The fares range from S$0.60 to S$1.50. Tickets can be purchased from a vending machine or from a booth. You will need your ticket to enter and exit the stations.

BUSES

➤ The bus system is fairly easy to use. All signs are in English. Buses run from 6 A.M. to 11:30 P.M. You will need exact change for your fare, which runs from S$0.30 to S$0.90.

FERRIES

➤ Most of the regularly scheduled ferries leave from the World Trade Center. Weekday departures are at 10 A.M. and 1:30 P.M. There are eight scheduled departures on Sundays and holidays for destinations such as St. John's and Kusu islands for swimming and picnics and Sentosa Island for theme parks. Check with your hotel for fees and return schedules.

Tipping

> The government actively discourages tipping.

> Hotels: Offer bellhops S$2.00 for extra services, but don't be surprised if they refuse to accept a tip.

> Restaurants: All restaurants, except small, family-run eateries, add a 10 percent service charge to your bill.

> Taxi drivers: Don't give anything except small change.

Business/Banking/Shopping Hours

> Business hours during the week are from 9 A.M. to 1 P.M. and from 2 P.M. to 5 P.M. Saturday hours are from 9 A.M. to 1 P.M.

> Banks are open during the week from 10 A.M. to 3 P.M. and from 11 A.M. to 4:30 P.M. Saturdays.

> Shops are open daily from 10:30 A.M. to 10 P.M.

Time to Eat

Breakfast is generally served from 7 to 8 A.M., lunch from noon to 1:30 P.M. (the typical office lunch hour is from 1:00 to 2:00 P.M.), and dinner from 7 to 9 P.M.

Toilets

Most restroom facilities will be Western-style, though you may occasionally come across an Eastern-style squat toilet. Bring your own tissues.

HOLIDAYS

Singapore's many holidays and festivals reflect its diverse culture. Listed here are the most important. Some are based on the lunar calendar, so the dates vary from year to year. Check those listed below that do not show a specific date to find out exactly when they are held

National Holidays

Government offices, banks, businesses, and schools are closed on these days.

➤ *January 1*
New Year's Day.

➤ *January/February*
Chinese New Year is the most important holiday in Singapore, and businesses are often closed for a week during the festivities. The Chingay Procession signifies the end of the holiday, when Orchard Road is closed to traffic to allow for a spectacular parade of floats, dancers, and acrobats.

➤ *February/March*
Hari Raya Puasa marks the end of the month of Ramadan, a period of fasting and devotion, during which Muslims through self-discipline reflect on their faith and its meaning.

➤ *March/April*
Good Friday.

➤ *May 1*
Labor Day.

➤ *May*
Hari Raya Haji commemorates the pilgrimage to Mecca. On this day the mosques are full of worshipers.

➤ *May*
Vesak Day celebrates the birth of the Buddha.

➤ *August 9*
National Day is celebrated with a spectacular parade at the National Stadium and fireworks at night. Admission is by ticket only.

➤ *October/November*
Deepavali, or the Hindu Festival of Lights, celebrates the victory of the legendary Rama, an incarnation of Vishnu, one of the Hindu trinity of gods, over the demon king Ravana. Oil lamps are lit outside of Hindu homes.

➤ *December 25*
Christmas Day.

Other Holidays and Festivals

➤ *January*
Ponggal, a southern Indian harvest festival, is celebrated at Sri Mariamman Temple, South Bridge Road.

➤ *June*
The Singapore Festival of the Arts is a biennial celebration of art, drama, dance, and music featuring artists from all over the world.

➤ *June*
The Dragon Boat Festival, which falls on the fifth day of the fifth lunar month, commemorates the suicide-by-drowning of the Chinese poet Ch'u Yuan, who was protesting a corrupt government. Everyone turns out to watch the dragon boat races held on the river. This is one of Singapore's most colorful celebrations. Teams from all over the world meet to compete at the World Invitational Dragon Boat Race. Colorful boats, frenzied rowers, pounding drums, and the ample availability of seasonal delicacies combine to make this an especially festive occasion.

➤ *July/August*
The Festival of the Hungry Ghosts is a Taoist celebration lasting thirty days. During this time the souls of the dead are free to wander in this world and must be appeased with offerings by the living.

➤ *September*
The Mooncake Festival is observed with local children parading through the streets carrying traditional lanterns. This is the only time of year you can purchase these ornate lanterns as souvenirs.

➤ *September/October*
The Navarathiri Festival celebrates Hindu deities at Chettiar Temple

on Tank Road for nine nights with traditional Indian music and
dances and a parade.

➤ *October/November*
The Festival of the Nine Emperor Gods offers colorful Chinese
operas, processions, and floats with images of the gods.

RECOMMENDED HOTELS, RESTAURANTS

The list below includes places we think would be comfortable for
women and, in the case of restaurants, suitable for entertaining business
clients. We have rated our hotel recommendations from $$ to $$$$,
with $$$$ being the most expensive (e.g., over S$300 per night).

Hotels

➤ *Mandarin Singapore ($$$$)*
333 Orchard Road
Singapore
Tel: 737-4411
Fax: 732-2361
Minuses:
• No in-room modem hook-up
• No courtesy airport transportation

➤ *Pan Pacific Hotel ($$$)*
7 Raffles Boulevard, Marina Square
Singapore
Tel: 336-8111
Fax: 339-1861
Plus:
• Full range of amenities

➤ *Sheraton Towers ($$$$)*
39 Scotts Road
Singapore
Tel: 737-6888
Fax: 737-1072

Minuses:
- No in-room modem hook-up
- No translation service
- No 24-hour cable TV news station
- No hairdresser
- No courtesy airport transportation

➤ *Shangri-La Hotel ($$$)*
22 Orange Grove Road
Singapore
Tel: 737-3644
Fax: 733-7220
Plus:
- Situated among lush tropical gardens.
Minus:
- No 24-hour cable TV news station
- No in-room checkout
- No garage
- No courtesy airport transportation

➤ *Hyatt Regency ($$$$)*
10-12 Scotts Road
Singapore
Tel: 733-1234
Fax: 732-1696
Plus:
- Regency Club floors with amenities for members
Minuses:
- No in-room modem hook-up
- No courtesy airport transportation

Restaurants

While in Singapore, it will be very worth your while to try some of the different cuisines offered from Chinese, Malay, and Indian cultures. One fun and easy way to see what is on offer is to go to one of the outdoor open-air food markets called "hawker" centers. These are all over Singapore. Browse from stall to stall to select and order the dishes you want, then take your "chit" to a picnic-style table. Servers will bring your dishes over to you.

Seafood lovers might also consider a casual meal at one of Singapore's major seafood restaurants, where you shop for your dinner with a grocery cart. Your "catch" will then be freshly cooked at your table. The local seafood favorite is chili crab.

SEAFOOD

➢ *UDMC Seafood Centre*
Block 1202-04, East Coast Parkway
Singapore
• Usually open from 11 A.M. to 1 A.M.; features eight seafood restaurants.

➢ *Long Beach Restaurant*
1018 East Coast Parkway #01-02
Singapore
Tel: 445-8833

INDIAN

➢ *Tandoor*
Holiday Inn Park View
11 Cavenagh Road
Singapore
Tel: 733-8333

➢ *Rang Mahal*
Hotel Imperial
1 Jalan Rumbia
Singapore
Tel: 737-1666

➢ *Banana Leaf Apollo*
69 Balestier Road
Tel: 293-8682
Singapore
• As the name says, meals are served on banana leaves.

➢ *Guan Hoe Soon Restaurant*
214 Joo Chiat Road
Singapore
Tel: 440-5650

MALAY

➤ *Bintang Timur Restaurant*
02-08/13 Far East Plaza
14 Scotts Road
Singapore
Tel: 235-4539

➤ *Nonya and Baba*
262 River Valley Road
Singapore
Tel: 734-1382

➤ *Aziza's*
36 Emerald Hill Road
Singapore
Tel: 235-1130

CHINESE

➤ *Prima Tower*
201 Keppel Road
Singapore
Tel: 272-8988
• Revolving restaurant that serves a variety of Peking cuisine.

➤ *Shang Palace*
Shangri-La Hotel
22 Orange Grove Road
Singapore
Tel: 737-3644
• Specializes in Cantonese dishes.

➤ *Prince Room*
Selegie Complex
275-285 Selegie Road
Singapore
Tel: 337-7141
• Hokkien cuisine is featured.

➤ *Cherry Garden*
Oriental Singapore

5 Raffles Avenue
Singapore
Tel: 338-0066
- Hunan dishes are served here.

➢ *Min Jiang Sichuan Restaurant*
Goodwood Park Hotel
22 Scotts Road
Singapore
Tel: 737-7411
- Noted for its Szechwan cuisine.

WHAT TO SEE AND DO

Changi Airport

If you are stuck waiting at the airport, you will find that this modern two-terminal facility offers more to do than any other airport in Asia and is an interesting place to explore.

➢ *Free Singapore Tour*
Changi Airport offers a free tour around the island for passengers with four-hour layovers. The motor coach tour covers East Coast Parkway, Benjamin Sheares Bridge, Chinatown, Clifford Pier, the Empress Place Museum (for a fifteen-minute stop), and Little India. There are two spots in the airport to catch the bus, which leaves at 2:30 and 4:30 P.M. daily.

➢ *Fitness Center*
There are two fitness centers located in the departures/transit lounge of each terminal. Each center has a gym, sauna, and shower rooms. Lockers are free.

➢ *Movie Theater*
There is a small movie theater in Terminal 1 that holds about seventy people. It is located on the third floor of the departures/transit lounge. Movies are shown at 5:30 and 8:00 P.M. daily. Admission is free.

➤ *Science Discovery Center*
There is a hands-on interactive science exhibit located on the third level of the departures/transit lounge in Terminal 2 that is fun for both adults and children.

➤ *Shopping*
There are ninety-four shops to investigate between the two terminals at Changi Airport.

➤ *Vidiwall*
A twenty-four-screen video wall in the departure/transit lounge shows music, sports, and documentary clips that highlight Singapore culture. Screenings are on from 7 A.M. to 1 A.M. daily.

➤ *Airport Information*
Telefigs is a twenty-four-hour interactive computer system that provides flight schedule and terminal and departure hall information.

Areas of Interest

Though Singapore is often criticized by tourists for being overly modern and clean, a map and a decent pair of walking shoes can take you to some interesting areas of town that still maintain their ethnic flavor.

➤ *Arab Street*
This area is like a bazaar, with shops selling basketware, batik, curry spices, textiles, and leather goods. Visit the gold-domed Sultan Mosque; if you are in shorts or a halter top you will not be allowed inside. Friday is the Moslem day of worship.

➤ *Bedok*
This is a large housing estate about a twenty-minute train ride from Orchard Road. It has been tagged "Gold Town" for its abundance of jewelry stores and goldsmiths. Clothing is sold here too, as well as a favorite sweet—"cocktail jelly"—shaved ice with fruit cocktail on top.

➤ *Bugis Village*
Visit this restored and laundered version of Bugis Street, where sailors and transvestites once drank and cavorted. Now beer gardens, restaurants, and shops attract visitors and locals alike.

➤ *Boat Quay and Clarke Quay*
Restored warehouses, filled with restaurants and boutiques, frame the banks of Singapore River. Watch street musicians, clowns and acrobats perform as you browse through arts-and-crafts stalls. Have dinner al fresco with a view of the river, or dine at one of the four restored barges moored here. The bridges across the river are illuminated at night, as is the statue of Raffles, the Parliament houses, and Empress Place.

➤ *Chinatown*
This district in the South Bridge and New Bridge area has many shops that offer both traditional and modern wares.

➤ *The New Ming Village*
Located at 32 Pandan Road, this shop west of downtown has reproductions of Ming and Ching porcelain for sale. You can watch as it is made. Admission is free.

➤ *Little India*
Walking distance from Chinatown and Arab Street, this area is interesting for its its elaborate Hindu temples and views of Indian women in colorful sarees selling spices.

Tours

➤ *Cruises*
Take a Chinese junk, modern cruiser, or charter vessel for a tour of Singapore from the river and the harbor. Most leave from Clifford Pier.

➤ *Riverboat Tours*
These 30-minute tours, which begin at Raffles Landing and wend their way on a historical voyage down the Singapore River, offer taped narration in English on the sights along the way.

➤ *Ferry Trips*
Plying their way from the World Trade Center to the outer islands of St. John's and Kusu, these tours offer visitors pleasant day-trip getaways. Take a swimsuit and a snack for a pleasant afternoon float in a lagoon.

Parks

➤ *Jurong BirdPark*
This sanctuary on Jurong Hill houses some 5,000 birds of 450 species from all over the world. Penguin Parade has an underground viewing window. Feeding times are 10:30 A.M. and 3:30 P.M. There are also Birds of Prey and All-Star Bird shows. Admission fee charged.

➤ *Botanical Gardens*
With its jungle, elegant landscaping, and greenhouses, these gardens demonstrate just how lush and tropical Singapore is. Located at Napier Street and Holland Road. Admission is free.

➤ *Chinese and Japanese Gardens*
The gardening styles of two prominent Asian cultures are featured here. The Chinese Garden is styled after the Sung Dynasty Beijing Summer Palace. A bridge links it to a traditional Japanese garden. Located on Yuan Ching Road. Admission fee charged.

➤ *Zoological Gardens*
Here's your chance to have breakfast or tea with an orangutan! Book the air- conditioned Zoo Express bus from your hotel to the Mandai Lake Road location. The package includes admission to the zoo and the Mandai Orchid Gardens.

➤ *Mandai Orchid Gardens*
Beautiful displays of a wide variety of orchids bloom all year round. Located on Mandai Lake Road next to the zoo. Admission fee charged.

Theme Parks

➤ *Haw Par Villa (Tiger Balm Gardens)*
Bizarre statues of Chinese mythological figures dot the grounds. The Spirits of the Orient Theatre offers a multimedia presentation of Chinese culture; the Creation of the World Theatre presents a three-dimensional show of the legend of Pan Go, creator of the world, and Nu War, creator of the human race. Other entertainments include puppet shows, a "Tales of China" boat ride, and the Wrath of Water Gods flume ride. Admission fee charged.

➤ *Sentosa Island*
Singapore's version of Disneyland includes Fantasy Island, Butterfly Park, VolcanoLand, Orchid Fantasy, and Underwater World theme parks. Also on site are the Night Safari and Asian Village, along with unique museums, gardens, nature reserves, and river cruises. Ferry over from the World Trade Center. Ask at your hotel for the Sentosa Discovery Package, which includes bus/train transfers and admission to most major attractions. You can also take a cable car from Mt. Faber to the island, from which you enjoy a panoramic view of the harbor and surrounding area.

➤ *Tang Dynasty City*
This is Asia's largest historical theme park. A re-creation of Chang-An, capital of seventh-century Tang China, it includes terracotta warrior statues, monkey god performances, and many other attractions. Located off Jalan Ahmad Ibrahim. Admission charged.

Evening Entertainment

Singapore has many places to eat, dance, and otherwise enjoy the evening. Since you may feel a bit uncomfortable in other Asian cities, you might want to exploit Singapore's reputation for safety to go out and get some much-needed R&R. Singapore has many movie theaters as well as karaoke bars. Dinner cruises and evening dinner-dance excursions leave from Clifford Pier. A selection of other recreations is included here, but your hotel will give you the most up-to-date information.

➤ *Singapore Symphony*
Concerts are held at Victoria Concert Hall. Check with your hotel concierge for the schedule.

➤ *Theaters*
Plays, musicals, and ballets are performed at the Drama Centre in Canning Rise and the Victoria Theatre in Empress Place. Consult the local newspapers or your hotel concierge for current productions.

➤ *Lido Palace*
Has bands, live shows, and disco dancing with dinner. Located at the Concorde Hotel Shopping Centre, Outram Road.

➤ *Neptune Theatre Restaurant*
Offers Cantonese cuisine and a cabaret at Collyer Quay.

> *Singa Inn Seafood*
> This restaurant spotlights an Asian cultural show with its "catch your own" seafood meals. Located at 920 East Coast Parkway.

> *Hard Rock Cafe*
> Located on Cuscaden Road, this eatery offers the same attractions as its New York, London, or Tokyo branch.

> *Flag and Whistle Pub*
> On Duxton Hill. A traditional English pub with billiards and darts. Bring your favorite cassette tape and they will play it.

> *Raffles Hotel*
> Always good for a drink. Soak in the atmosphere at the famous Long Bar in this faithfully renovated landmark (notorious for creating the Singapore Sling). Asian finger foods and English dishes are served here in a tropical cane-and-rattan setting. Bowls of peanuts top the tables, while shells litter the floor.

Temples and Mosques

There are many sacred buildings representing the great religions of the world in and about Singapore, due to the city's diverse cultural heritage. See the discussions, above, about Arab Street and Little India, for example.

TEMPLE ETIQUETTE

> Remove your shoes before entering mosques or Hindu temples.

> In Hindu temples, refrain from touching statues or paintings and from smoking.

> Remove your hat before entering a Chinese temple. You will seldom need to remove your shoes.

> Don't take photographs without permission.

WORTH VISITING

> *Sri Mariamman Temple*
> This is Singapore's oldest Hindu temple, site of Thimithi fire-walking ceremony during the fall. Located on South Bridge Road.

➤ *Sultan Mosque*
Near Arab Street, this golden-domed building is the main focus of Muslim worship in Singapore.

➤ *Temple of 1,000 Lights*
Featured here is a colorful, nearly fifty-foot statue of the Buddha, with paintings depicting the important stages in his life. Located on Race Course Road.

SHOPPING

Singapore is a duty-free port and an Asian shopping center for both authentic and knock-off brand goods. Many business travelers come to Singapore for good deals on name-brand products.

Shopping Tips

While there are bargains to be had, beware of potential scams:

➤ Taxi drivers and guides are often paid to bring customers to certain shops. Be firm with the driver about where you want to go.

➤ The only assurance you have that the item you have purchased is real is the credibility of the shop. Get all warranties and verify that they apply in your country.

➤ Check and make sure items purchased in Singapore (crocodile, for example) are not illegal to bring into your home country.

Malls and Markets

➤ *Orchard Road*
This is Singapore's trendiest shopping street, with just about every name-brand store and commodity you might be looking for.

➤ *Marina Square*
This three-level shopping mall off Raffles Boulevard has food and clothing outlets, electronics stores, and an open-air food court.

USEFUL MALAY PHRASES		
English	*Malay*	*Pronunciation*
Good morning	Selamat pagi	S'lahmaht pahghee
Good afternoon	Selamat tengah hari	S'lahmaht teng-gah ha-ree
Good evening	Selamat malam	S'lahmaht mahlahm
Goodnight	Selamat malam	S'lahmaht mahlahm
Goodbye	Selamat tinggal	S'lahmaht teenggal
Please	Minta	Minta
Thank you	Terima kasih	T'rreema kasseehh
Excuse me	Minta maafkan	Minta ma'ahf-kahn
Yes	Ya	Yah
No	Tidak	Teedah'
I understand	Saya mengerti	Sahya m'ng-rr-tee
I don't understand	Saya tidak mengerti	Sahya teedah' m'ng-rr-tee
Does anyone here speak English?	Bolehkah kamu beibalasa inggris?	Bo-leh-kah ka-moo bei-ba-la-sa engres?

> *Chinatown Centre*
Art and handicraft shops, clothing outlets, and food stalls are found in this complex on New Bridge Road.

> *Park Mall*
This shopping center on Penang Lane is renowned for its boutiques and food outlets.

> Singapore also has skilled tailors who are very reasonable. If you are planning a longer stay or will be making several trips to Singapore, you may want to bring your favorite dress and have duplicates made in lighter fabrics. The cost will often work out to be less than the purchase of a new dress back home.

9 | South Korea

On my first visit to South Korea, I traveled with six men. I was the manager. Koreans, I think, are a lot like the Japanese. They have many similarities and many of the formalities. One thing male visitors like to do is to go to hostess bars and nightclubs after business meetings. I could tell my hosts were worried about me. They wanted to make sure I was happy and would not be offended by the hostess bar experience they had planned. In these bars hostesses feed you hors d'oeuvres, help you drink your drink, and dance as well as chat with you. They dress very sexily too. I really did not know what to expect but wanted to stick with my team. My Korean counterparts were so worried about what to do that they asked for my advice. I said that since they made the plans and I had never been to a Korean after-hours bar, perhaps we should go. So we all went. Well, sure enough, when we got there, all those things I had read about were visible. I was feeling uncomfortable. My hosts, very conscious of my response, asked me again what I wanted to do. I tried to make light of it and said, "Well, I guess the women will have to feed me too." (But I did not dance with the hostesses.) In the end they shortened the night considerably and suggested that I let them know where I would like to spend the next night out. (Austin, Texas)

In South Korea, as in other Confucian cultures, woman's role is one of deference to men. It is her duty to produce a male heir and manage the family for the comfort of her husband, father, and sons. Among the Four Tigers, South Korea is still the most rigidly traditional. However, at the beginning of the Yi (Choson) Dynasty in the fourteenth century, there is evidence that women had more power. During the Shilla Kingdom (57 B.C. –A.D. 668), there were in fact three ruling queens, one of whom was noted for her outstanding leadership ability. Throughout Korean history women have distinguished themselves in the arts, but the first girls' school did not open until 1886.

In modern times, the number of Korean women entering the work force has increased rapidly, particularly over the last decade, with women accounting for 40 percent of the industrial work force as of 1990.[1] This is expected to reverse if reunification with the North occurs, since large numbers of North Korean males are expected to take their place.

In general, women's wages are about 53 percent those of men. Wage controls have forced many women to work as cocktail waitresses rather than accept lower factory wages and poorer working conditions, and most women still quit their jobs when they marry or have a child. It will be some time before women in South Korea receive full acceptance in the work force.

Nevertheless, Korean women are more visibly assertive than their Asian sisters. While they are careful to protect male egos, they state their position more openly and directly than other Asian women. As more women enter the work force, their choices will begin to affect the market more. There will, for example, be more demand for convenience goods, most of which are produced right in South Korea. The country's population growth, however, appears to be slowing, and this will further affect the labor pool. Employers have called for the admission of foreign labor, but this has not yet been widely accepted.

Today, Western businesswomen complain that the Koreans are the most blatantly sexist group in Asia. Not only do they feel that Korean women are discriminated against, but that they also appear, on some occasions, to be denigrated. One of our interviewees recalled that when she attended a Korean cultural show with her hosts, she casually mentioned how beautiful Korean women were. Her host responded, "Yeah, they sure are. But my wife is ugly.'" She was shocked to hear this apparent put down of his wife, whom she later learned was quite beautiful. Why do Korean men say such things? Some say that it is an expression of modesty due to their Confucian upbringing, and that this man was truly thrilled to have such a beautiful wife. He could not, however, brag about his lucky situation, so had to humble himself by saying she was ugly.

Unmarried Western women traveling to South Korea will often be asked about their single status. It is unusual for Korean women to travel unescorted and, from the Korean male standpoint, women should be married and home by their mid-twenties. Married women with children may be asked why they are traveling on business. The assumption here is that the husband is not a good provider and therefore she needs to work.

Traveling to South Korea for businesswomen of Asian descent can be even more uncomfortable than for women of other racial backgrounds. An Asian woman must be very confident and assertive, but not aggressive. If an Asian businesswoman does not display confidence, her Korean contacts may view her as "a typical Korean woman" and withhold their respect. At the same time, our Asian interviewees advised, an Asian woman must not be too aggressive, since she may be subjected to derogatory comments about her double life—a professional woman and a wife and mother with a neglected family and henpecked husband at home.

Remember that as a Western businesswoman and a foreigner your situation will be different from that of Korean women. If you are one of the first Western businesswomen to visit your Korean contacts, you may find yourself viewed as a star. One woman we interviewed told us how many Koreans, even people she didn't know, had left messages at her hotel asking to meet her. As the first Western businesswoman in their area, they were quite curious to see a "live one." Handle this sort of attention graciously. Remember that being viewed as an oddity can make you as effective, if not more effective, than your male counterparts.

DOING BUSINESS IN SOUTH KOREA

The South Korean business environment is often compared to the Japanese business environment. South Korea's business is dominated by large conglomerates called *chaebol*, which are very similar to Japanese *zaibatsu*. These mammoth conglomerates, worth $50 billion and more, cover multiple product lines from cars to consumer electronics. Due to the size of most *chaebol*, the companies within it may act independently of each other.

Like Japan, South Korea has a homogeneous population, is geographically isolated to a certain degree, was opened to the West at a relatively late date, and is characterized by strong, traditional family ties. Despite these similarities, South Korea's and Japan's cultures are quite different. Koreans will be quick to tell you this if you try to compare the two. The Korean people are more direct, emotional, and confrontational than the Japanese, and the Confucian influence in the work environment is stronger in Korea than in Japan.

When you conduct a meeting in South Korea, you may notice that Korean businessmen seem loud and aggressive—much more so than businessmen in the other three Asian Tigers. This is simply how they communicate. Although Koreans are very conscious about creating a harmonious atmosphere and saving face, Westerners often perceive their style as blunt and abrupt, since they tend to be brusque with people they don't know. If you are not in their inner circle, there is no reason for them to be very friendly. This is not always the case, but it has occurred frequently enough to remark on here.

Koreans conduct business formally; if you are comfortable working in Japan you can easily maneuver in South Korea. When conducting business in South Korea, keep in mind how important it is to establish harmony and to save face. Koreans refer to their feelings or their mood by the word *kibun*. They do not like to unload any negative feelings on another's *kibun*. They find it difficult to share bad news and will attempt to soften it. Like other Asians, Koreans will appear to laugh or smile during difficult times to mask their innermost feelings.

Koreans are very hospitable. Culturally, they are adept at gracious entertaining and gift giving and can be overwhelmingly kind. Overall, Korean culture is very emotional. Koreans may express their emotion through warmth, loyalty, and compassion. Although most Koreans tend to hide their emotions from the outside world, they are quite different with people with whom they become close. In a business setting, this warmth may be expressed through large gifts, dinners, steadfast loyalty, and additional business.

Korean negotiators may start off with an extreme position, expecting to back down after you have stated your position. If this is the approach they are taking, above all, remain patient and courteous and hold to your position firmly but flexibly during the business sessions. In negotiations, emotional considerations are often more important than Western-style logic. Try to understand the underlying motivation for the other side's position and emotional maneuvering.

Overall, South Korea is the most difficult country for women to work in of all the Asian Tigers. But conducting business with Koreans can be very challenging and rewarding for a woman. The Koreans are vocally more chauvinistic than their Asian counterparts, and thus create tension and perhaps may even shock women who do business with them. Koreans tend to be more direct and open in some ways; as in the West, they use eye contact more frequently and are more prone to expressing their feelings. They are more apt to openly express their unhappiness at working with women. Many Western women report that, compared with Japan, where the hostility is almost never overt, the openness of Korean men is easier to deal with because the problem is out on the table and can be dealt with proactively.

Taking a cue from the Korean men, you as a woman doing business in Korea can be more assertive in Korea than you might dare to be elsewhere in Asia. Having addressed the female-in-business issue, you can move on to other business matters. Through positioning, a good understanding of the business at hand, and solid leadership, you will be able to dispel any reservations your Korean counterparts may have about working with a Western woman. We recall that when a Korean businessman came to visit us in the United States and we reviewed our company's organization charts with him, he was surprised to learn that there were women at each level of the organization and that the general manager was a woman. He said, quite openly, that this situation would never occur in South Korea, nor would he want it to. But once we had established that this was the way our organization was run and that it wasn't going to change, he quickly accepted it and we moved on to a more productive business conversation.

South Korea is internationalizing quickly, and there is increasing acceptance of women in the work force, especially among younger Koreans. But even though the behavior is changing, attitudes will take a little longer to change.

WHAT WOMEN SAY

The Tantrum
We had to cancel a business proposal with a vendor from South Korea. The team (men and women) arranged a meeting at our company in the U.S. to tell them. They arrived and the meeting was going well. Then, as

the highest-ranking person and elected spokesperson, I had to break the news to them about our forthcoming plans. I told them that this decision was part of the business plan and that they were not being singled out. One of the Korean men jumped up and started yelling at me. He was having a tantrum! I stopped and sat there for a moment and let him continue his ranting and raving. Then I asked him if he was finished so that we could continue the meeting. With that I calmly continued the meeting without any further interruptions. (San Jose, California)

No Response
I was in a meeting in South Korea. It appeared as though the Korean businessmen had never dealt with a businesswoman before. I recall asking a question and no one answering me. Instead there was silence and some uncomfortable looks. In an attempt to help me out, my male colleague re-asked the question. They immediately answered him. Later, the Koreans asked a question for which I was the appropriate person to respond. When I did respond, they did not acknowledge what I had said but looked toward my male colleague for a response. This time my male colleague said, "Jane is the appropriate person to answer your question." (Cupertino, California)

Translator?
The status of women in South Korea is very low, much lower than in Japan. As an Asian, I felt that I was being looked down on. I feel Korean men treat Asian women with less respect than Western women, so I am never really at ease in South Korea because they make me feel very aware of our gender differences and their expectations. For example, I speak Korean and use it in social situations only. During one meeting, I found that my Korean counterparts wanted me to act as a translator and not as the engineer I am. In the beginning, I helped out a little bit but once I realized their intentions, I stopped. I started to talk back to them in English just like everyone else and said I had trouble understanding some of the words and could not be of much help. (Singapore)

Credibility Tactics
I organized a meeting at our home base in the U.S. with our South Korean counterparts. There would be three Korean men visiting with us. On the U.S. side, we were three women and two men. Our meeting was going very well. I answered the issues that were mine and referred

other issues to my team members as appropriate. It soon became obvious that one Korean man in particular was questioning all responses made by the women in the group. Perhaps subconsciously noting this, one of my male team members took over the meeting in an effort to stop the questioning and continue the meeting. The other women and I immediately called a break. We reviewed the situation and our roles once again. We felt that even if it took all day, each person had to keep his or her role and continually defer to the appropriate business representative when questions were asked. We felt that taking the time now to establish our credibility as a team and as women was more important than getting through the meeting. And it worked. (Colorado Springs, Colorado)

The Tea-Serving Thing

I am a female Asian-American engineer. At a meeting in the U.S., while on my way to the restroom during a break, I bumped into some newly arrived South Korean suppliers who were to join the meeting after the break. I greeted them in Korean since I am bilingual. I then showed them where we were meeting. When I returned to the table, the meeting had started up again. One of the Koreans leaned over to me and whispered in Korean if I would bring him some tea. I pointed out the service that had been set up in the back of the room Western style and whispered that he was free to have tea any time he wished. (San Diego, California)

GENERAL ETIQUETTE

From our observations and those of businesspeople we interviewed, the points mentioned below were felt to be of particular importance for doing business in South Korea. Refer also to the more general discussion in Chapter 2.

➢ Koreans view themselves as being unique. Do not compare them to the Chinese or the Japanese; they will remind you that they are Korean.

➢ When you are walking on sidewalks and stairways, keep to the left.

➢ Western women tend to be larger than Korean women, an observation that may be pointed out to you with great matter-of-factness by both Korean men and women.

➢ Allow people to pass in front of you rather than behind you.

➢ Korean women tend to walk in groups and hold hands or walk arm in arm. Men often walk arm in arm in groups. This is a sign of camaraderie and nothing more.

➢ Doors are not usually held open for women, and men typically enter and exit before women. This does not mean that you have to follow men, but be aware that if a male enters before you do, he is only following local etiquette.

➢ Do not eat in the street or blow your nose in public. Throw used tissues into a garbage pail, not into your purse.

➢ Pushing and bumping in streets, subways, and department stores is normal and accepted; groping is not. There are now "women only" cars on the subway if you feel that you will be uncomfortably jostled during your journeys.

➢ Koreans eat a lot of garlic. It is impolite to remark on the smell of garlic in the country and people.

➢ You will see a lot of Koreans chewing a very strong mint gum to mask the garlic odor on their breath. You may want to keep strong mints with you too.

Body Language

Koreans use eye contact when they are speaking with you, since this is considered more direct and a sign of trustworthiness. This is unlike other Asians, who avoid eye contact because it seems challenging and impolite.

Koreans do not appreciate an overly outgoing style. They will limit direct physical contact to a handshake. Although they stand closer to each other when talking than Westerners do, they do not touch each other.

➢ Public displays of affection between the sexes, such as a hug or a kiss, is discouraged.

➢ Keep your hands in full view when you're talking to people; this signifies trust. Avoid putting them in your pockets or behind your back.

➤ If you want to cross your legs, put one knee over the other and point your soles and toes downward, or keep your legs together with your feet on the floor. It is impolite to show the soles of your shoes to another person.

➤ Do not point at anyone with a single finger. To beckon someone, hold your arm out, palm down, and wave your fingers up and down.

➤ Korean women usually cover their mouths when they laugh; it is considered improper for them to show their teeth.

BUSINESS ETIQUETTE

Contacts

➤ Have a mutually respected third party introduce you in advance; Korean businesspeople are reluctant to meet with people they do not know.

➤ Though Koreans are more direct and initially appear to be more open than the Japanese in business settings, they place just as much importance on trust and the establishment of a comfortable relationship.

➤ If you intend to conduct long-term business in Korea, plan on making frequent trips to build your relationship. Face-to-face contact is always preferred to faxes and e-mail.

➤ The best business approach in Korea is to be polite and somewhat formal. As the relationship develops, you will find that you and they will relax more and become more open.

Greetings/Addresses

➤ Salutations and expressions of appreciation are very important to Koreans. These are usually accompanied with a slight bow of the head.

➤ Bring plenty of business cards. Have them translated into Korean on the back.

➤ Business cards are exchanged with two hands, usually at the beginning of the meeting before you sit down. Repeat the name of the person you are meeting and express a genuine interest in his title and company.

➤ After you are seated, place the business cards one at a time on the table in front of you, arranging them in the same order as the people sitting opposite you. This will help you remember their names.

➤ If an introduction to you is overlooked, politely but assertively offer your business card to your Korean hosts and introduce yourself with a handshake. This will emphasize your participation in the meeting.

➤ If you know a person's title, use it in your salutation when you correspond with them.

➤ Koreans respect age. Greet the senior people in the room first. Junior persons will most likely bow to you.

➤ You may be asked your age and marital status. This is so your Korean counterparts can more easily determine their position in relation to you. (Being older holds more status than being younger; being married gives you a slightly higher status than being single.) You do not, however, have to respond.

➤ Initiate a handshake with Korean men if it is not offered to you.

➤ When you are introduced to a Korean, the family name is usually given first. This is used by persons outside the family. This is followed by a two-part given name, which is used by parents with their children.

➤ Typically, Koreans do not use their first names in business, since this is considered impolite. Address your counterparts by their last names, such as Mr. Kim, unless they offer their first name. Some use Americanized first names and offer this name for you to use.

➤ The four most popular surnames in South Korea are Lee, Choi, Park, and Kim. Make a note of your contacts' full names and company titles when you are visiting South Korea in case you need to look them up in a telephone directory.

➤ You may be addressed by your first name, since this is how women are addressed in South Korea, or by your last name. This will usually depend on how you are introduced. In a formal business situation, it is better to be addressed by your last name.

➤ Women are either Miss or Mrs. Ms. is not used.

➤ Although the situation is changing, women play secondary roles. It is unlikely that you will be working with women at the managerial level.

➤ Many older Koreans speak Japanese, which was taught during the Japanese Occupation from 1910–45. English is often used in business, though not as much as in the other Tiger countries.

➤ Avoid talking or laughing loudly in any situation; it is considered to be rude.

Meetings/Negotiations

➤ Be punctual for business meetings; this shows respect. As a general rule, Koreans are punctual in business. In social settings, you may find your Korean counterparts can be a little late.

➤ Prepare an agenda. Find out which people will be attending, and match them rank for rank.

➤ Assign someone to take notes. Review the notes at the end of the meeting to make sure both sides are in agreement. Then make copies so that the appropriate parties can follow up on any items that have not been resolved or need more discussion.

➤ Wait to sit until your host invites you to be seated.

➤ If you are offered tea, coffee, or soda, usually before the meeting begins, accept the beverage with both hands.

➤ Use the first meeting to build your relationship and establish a working rapport. It is best not to launch directly into your business proposal.

➤ Make sure that you are well prepared before entering into negotiations. The Koreans will be prepared to cover many aspects of the business with you. Have a clear understanding of what you want, your must-haves, give-aways, and your fall-back position.

➤ Retaining face is important. Instead of saying no to your request, your Korean business contacts may say yes (even if they don't mean it) to avoid upsetting you. Accordingly, the best approach is not to ask yes-no questions, but rather open-ended questions that will require some dialogue between you. Observe your Korean contacts closely, since you may be able to spot nonverbal clues that indicate they do not agree with a point.

➤ A yes response or a smile may mean merely "I hear and understand you." Draw out the discussion further to find out what their position is.

➤ Koreans, businesspeople included, express frustration and anger much more freely than other Asians. You will find more expression in their speech and even outbursts in your interchanges with them.

➤ If Koreans laugh in situations considered inappropriate in the West, it is usually to hide their feelings.

➤ If a Korean has "lost face," he may react by becoming very stiff and formal.

➤ In a meeting with Western businesspeople, Koreans generally speak to each other in Korean. This should not be considered impolite.

➤ If emotions get out of hand during the meeting, politely suggest that it would be best to continue the meeting after a short break.

➤ If there are continual emotional outbreaks during the meeting, ignore these tactics and move on calmly as if they had not occurred.

ATTIRE

Koreans believe that they dress better than Taiwanese but not as flashy as the people in Hong Kong. Since South Korea has a conservative Confucian culture and is probably the most difficult country for women to gain credibility in, it is important that you dress conservatively and modestly in business settings. This means well-made, standard business suits. Wear a basic skirt suit in a conservative color, such as navy, and appropriate business shoes. You should wear hose, even during the hot summer months. Avoid wearing bright colors, loud prints, or large pieces of jewelry.

➤ Plan to wear woolen suits, heavy coats, and sturdy shoes, gloves, and scarves during the winter, which is very cold with occasional snow. Lightweight suits are appropriate in spring and summer, which can be very hot and humid. There is a rainy season in July and August, so bring an umbrella with you.

GIFT ETIQUETTE

➤ Gifts are usually presented at the first meeting. If you bring gifts, present them after your host has given you one.

➤ If visiting your home office in Korea, a bottle of Scotch whiskey is especially appreciated.

➤ Use both hands to present or receive a gift. Gifts are set aside to be opened at a later time. Refer to what you have received with a polite thank you the next day if you see the gift giver or, if you don't, follow up with a personalized thank-you note when you get back home.

➤ Don't give an expensive gift, since your Korean business contacts will feel obliged to return your gift in kind.

➤ Items with your company logo will generally be warmly received, as will baskets of food and specialties from your local area.

➤ Clocks, because of the sound of the word for clock in Chinese, are considered to represent death in Chinese cultures. Conversely, they are "good luck" business gifts in South Korea.

➤ Don't give four of anything. The number four, because of its sound in Korean, is a bad luck number.

➤ Wrap your gifts in a muted patterned, floral, or monotone-colored paper.

DINING ETIQUETTE

> Business entertaining generally takes place at restaurants and bars. South Koreans usually do not entertain business visitors at home, although if you are invited to someone's home it means he or she considers you a very good friend.

> South Koreans do not split the bill. If you initiate the meal, you are assumed to be the host and are therefore responsible for picking up the tab.

> The business dinner is part of the business meeting. It is important for women to attend these dinners.

> Men will use toothpicks at the table. Women usually don't.

> Traditionally, South Korean dinners are quiet, but most Koreans will make an effort to talk to be properly attentive to their guests.

> During meals, it is best to stick to broad topics such as sports or world events. Other good topics for conversation include South Korea's cultural traditions, its scenic beauty, sports, especially the Olympics, and the histories of your companies.

> Avoid discussing socialism, communism, domestic politics, unions and uprisings, trade friction, spouses, and comparisons of South Korea with other Asian cultures. Discussing family can be uncomfortable. Traditionally, Koreans prefer sons to daughters. If you ask about children, you might find they speak positively about their male children but express regret about having daughters.

> Koreans may ask you rather personal questions. Prepare standard nonconfrontational answers or remain silent to show that they are not appropriate.

> After dinner, your hosts may wish to entertain the male guests at one of Seoul's very expensive *kisaeng* houses or salons, where women entertain male guests with conversation, music, and even caresses while they drink and snack. Women may not appreciate this sort of entertainment and may wish to bow out. If the group wants to stick together, suggest a more appropriate alternative.

➤ Wives do not attend business dinners or events in South Korea. Do not bring your spouse or ask your counterparts to bring theirs.

TRAVEL ADVISORY

General Information

South Korea, formally called the Republic of Korea, occupies the southern half of a mountainous peninsula extending southward from eastern Asia. In 1953, at the end of the Korean War, it was separated from North Korea by a demilitarized zone. South Korea had a population of 44,056,087, according to the 1993 census, and a population growth rate of 0.9% in 1994. It is governed by President Kim Young Sam, with the next elections to be held in 1996. The Democratic Liberal Party (DLP) is currently the leading party.

Business Notes

South Korea developed an export-driven economy fostered by a dynamic entrepreneurial society. Its principal trading partners are the United States, Japan, and Germany. South Korea's real GDP growth rate was 8.4% in 1994. For information, contact:

Korea Trade (KOTRA)
1 California Street, Suite 1905
San Francisco, CA 94111
Tel: (415) 434-8400

Currency

The South Korean unit of currency is the won (KW). There were about KW760 to one U.S. dollar at the time of this printing. You can obtain money at hotels and banks, where you can also cash your travelers checks. Major credit cards can be used at hotels and the larger shops and restaurants.

SOUTH KOREA HIGH AND LOW TEMPERATURES IN FAHRENHEIT (F) AND CENTIGRADE (C)			
	High		*Low*
JAN	32°F 0°C	6°F	−14°C
FEB	37°F 3°C	20°F	−7°C
MAR	46°F 8°C	29°F	−2°C
APR	63°F 17°C	41°F	5°C
MAY	72°F 22°C	51°F	11°C
JUN	81°F 27°C	60°F	16°C
JUL	84°F 29°C	70°F	21°C
AUG	88°F 31°C	72°F	22°C
SEP	79°F 26°C	59°F	15°C
OCT	66°F 19°C	44°F	7°C
NOV	52°F 11°C	32°F	0°C
DEC	37°F 3°C	20°F	−7°C

Electricity/Electronics

South Korean electricity runs on a current of 110 volts and uses the VHS system for VCRs.

Entry and Departure

Visitors must hold a valid passport. You may also need to get a letter of guarantee from your company. Be able to show enough money for your visit and a return air ticket.

Visas are not required of tourists holding a valid U.S. passport for a stay of up to fifteen days in the Republic of Korea if they are en route to another destination in Asia. Business travelers are required to obtain a visa before entry from their local Republic of Korea Consulate Office. U.S. passport holders may obtain multiple-entry visas for sixty months for no fee. Contact:

Embassy of the Republic of Korea
Consular Division
600 Virginia Avenue, N.W., Suite 208
Washington, D.C. 20037
Tel: (202) 939-5660

➤ The airport departure tax is KW8,000 for international destinations, KW2,000 for domestic destinations.

Climate

South Korea has four seasons. Spring is windy. Summer is short and humid, with most rain occurring during this time. The hottest months are July and August with 80 percent humidity. This is the monsoon season. Typhoons with high winds and heavy rains can be expected in the south in late summer or early fall. Autumn is long and pleasant. In general, the best traveling months are April, May, June, September, and October, when the weather is very comfortable and there is very little rain. Winter is long, cold, and dry with relatively light snowfall.

Public Transportation

TAXIS

There are three types of taxis in Seoul: regular taxis, "88" taxis, and hotel taxis. Regular taxis are usually painted yellow and green and can be picked up at taxi stands along the major streets. The "88" cabs, which are roomier and more expensive, are also available at taxi stands. Hotel or tourist taxis are secured at hotels. The initial fare for hotel taxis is considerably higher than for the other two types. Carry a business card with the address of your destination to show the taxi driver, and a card with your hotel's name and address for your return.

Taxis are shared during busy times. A taxi will pick up a few passengers who are all heading in the same direction.

TRAINS

Trains are a safe alternative to express buses for intercity travel, since signs are written in the roman alphabet and stop maps are posted. Tickets can be purchased at automatic vending machines (bring change with you) or station ticket windows. Hold on to your ticket; you need it to enter and exit the stations. The trains will be crowded, particularly during commute hours. If this makes you feel uncomfortable, look for "women-only" cars.

BUSES

Bus services are inexpensive and easy to find. Getting on the right bus and off at the right stop can be difficult for foreigners, however, since all signs and directions are in Korean.

SUBWAYS

Seoul's rapidly expanding subway transports 3.6 million commuters a day between the hours of 5 A.M. and 12:30 A.M. These, too, are crowded and have "women only" cars.

Tipping

> ➤ Tips are not expected in Korea. When in doubt, don't tip.

> ➤ Hotels: Most add a 10 percent service charge to your bill.

> ➤ Restaurants: Bills usually include a 10 percent tip.

> ➤ Taxis: You don't need to tip; but if the driver helped with your luggage or provided an extra service, give him about 750 won.

> ➤ Porters: Tip about 250 won per piece of luggage.

> ➤ Barbers and beauticians: Tip about 15 percent.

> ➤ Chambermaids and cloakroom attendants: Tip about 750 won.

Business/Banking/Shopping Hours

> ➤ Business hours during the week in South Korea's major cities are from 9 A.M. to 6 P.M. in good weather and to 5 P.M. in the winter (November to March). Government offices are open on Saturday from 9 A.M. to 1 P.M.

> ➤ Banks are open from 9:30 A.M. until 4:30 P.M. weekdays and until 1:30 P.M. Saturday.

> ➤ Major department stores are open from about 10:30 A.M. to 7:30 P.M. daily, and street markets are open from early morning to the late evening.

Time to Eat

➤ Breakfast is generally served from 7:30 to 9 A.M., lunch from noon to 2 P.M. (the usual business lunch hour is between 12:30 and 1:30 P.M.), and dinner from 6 to 8 P.M.

Toilets

➤ You will find Western toilets in all large hotels and most commercial areas. However, you may also come across an Asian-style squat toilet. Watch your hem and carry tissue with you.

HOLIDAYS

Some holidays in South Korea are based on the lunar calendar, so the dates they are celebrated vary from year to year. Check those listed below that do not show a specific date to find out exactly when they are held.

National Holidays

Government offices, banks, businesses and schools are closed on these days.

➤ *January 1–2*
New Year's is the biggest holiday in South Korea. The most important tradition of the holidays is to bow deeply in gratitude to one's elders and ancestors.

➤ *January/February*
Lunar New Year.

➤ *March 1*
Independence Movement Day commemorates the March 1919 independence movement against Japanese colonial rule. There is an annual reading of the Korean Declaration of Independence.

➤ *April 5*
Arbor Day, a tree-planting day, is based on the belief that anything planted on this day will grow well.

➤ *April/May*
Buddha's Birthday is celebrated on the eighth day of the fourth lunar month with an evening parade. Many people buy lanterns to hang at the Buddhist temples.

➤ *May 5*
Children's Day is marked by many programs for children, who are allowed to do as they please on this day

➤ *June 6*
Memorial Day honors South Koreans who died in war.

➤ *July 17*
Constitution Day commemorates the adoption of the Constitution for the Republic of Korea in 1948.

➤ *August 15*
Liberation Day celebrates Korea's freedom from the Japanese in 1945 and the beginning of the Republic of Korea in 1948.

➤ *September/October*
Chusok, celebrated on the fifteenth day of the eighth lunar month, is South Korea's Thanksgiving Day, also called the Harvest Moon Festival.

➤ *October 3*
National Foundation Day commemorates the birthday of the legendary Tan Gun, who is said to have established Korea in 2333 B.C.

➤ *December 25*
Christmas Day.

Other Holidays and Festivals

➤ *March and September*
Sokchonje is a Confucian ceremony celebrated in Seoul honoring Confucius, his disciples, and other great Korean and Chinese sages. It is held in the Hall of the Great Sages at Sungkyunkwan University.

➤ *April*
King Tanjong Festival, held in Kangwon-do, is a ceremony of traditional music and dance performed to honor King Tanjong of the Yi Dynasty.

➤ *May (1st Sunday)*
Chongmyo Taeje, also called the Royal Shrine Rites, is a festival that
pays homage to the kings and queens of the Choson Dynasty. It is
held in Seoul at Chongmyo Shrine and celebrated with costume,
court music, and dance.

➤ *End of May*
The Arang Festival at Miryan, Kyongsamnan-do, honors Arang, a
Shilla heroine lauded for her marital fidelity. There is a beauty con-
test each year to choose Miss Arang, as well as a ceremony and traditional folk games.

➤ *October 9*
Hangul Day celebrates the creation of the Korean *hangul* alphabet
in 1443.

➤ *October/November*
The Kaech'on Arts Festival at Chinju in Kyongsangnam-do high-
lights local cultural activities such as Chinese poetry, calligraphy,
music and drama performances, and bullfights.

RECOMMENDED HOTELS, RESTAURANTS

The list below includes places we think would be comfortable for women
and, in the case of restaurants, suitable for entertaining business clients.
We have rated our hotel recommendations from $$ to $$$$, with $$$$
being the most expensive (i.e., over KW112,000 per night).

Hotels

➤ *Shilla Hotel ($$$$)*
202, 2-ga Changch'ung-dong
Chung-gu, Seoul
Tel: (02) 233-3131
Fax: (02) 233-5073
Plus:
• Sits on 23 acres of land
Minuses:

- No modem hook-up
- No 24-hour cable TV news station
- No garage

➤ *Grand Hyatt ($$$$)*
747-7 Hannam-dong
Yongsan-gu, Seoul
Tel: (02) 797-1234
Fax: (02) 798-6953
Pluses:
- Convenient location
- Regency Floor (premier floor) with amenities for members
Minuses:
- No non-smoking rooms
- No courtesy airport transportation

➤ *Intercontinental Hotel ($$$$)*
159-8 Samsong-dong
Kangnam-gu, Seoul
Tel: (02) 555-5656 or 800-332-4246
Fax: (02) 552-6422
Plus:
- Convenient location
Minuses:
- No computer rentals
- No 24-hour cable TV news station
- No non-smoking rooms
- No courtesy airport transportation

➤ *Hilton International ($$$$)*
395, 5-ga, Namdaemun-no
Chung-gu, Seoul
Tel: (02) 753-7788
Fax: (02) 754-2510
Pluses:
- Adjacent to convention center
- Extensive fitness facilities

➤ *Sheraton Walker Hill ($$$$)*
San 21, Kwangjang-dong
Songdong-ku, Seoul

Tel: (02) 453-0121
Fax: (02) 452-6867
Minus:
- No in-room checkout

➤ *Lotte ($$$$)*
1 Sogong-dong
Chung-gu, Seoul
Tel: (02) 771-1000
Fax: (02) 752-3758
Minus:
- No in-room checkout

Restaurants

Most of the major hotels in South Korea have a wide selection of Korean and international restaurants. They are generally very good and convenient choices for business lunches or dinners. Following are a few suggestions for restaurants located outside of hotels.

➤ *Seokparang*
125, Hongje-dong
Chongno-gu, Seoul
Tel: (02) 395-2500
- This atmospheric restaurant, in a renovated villa, specializes in royal dishes like those served to the ancient kings and nobles.

➤ *Soo Yeon*
105, Myongnyun-dong
Chongno-gu, Seoul
Tel: (02) 741-3451
- This old Korean house has been converted into a restaurant. It features traditional Korean foods in an intimate environment.

➤ *Waryongdong*
140-2, Waryong-dong
Chongno-gu, Seoul
Tel: (02) 764-4435
- This place specializes in *kuk-su-chon-gol*—noodles, meat, and vegetables boiled together in a large metal container at your table.

➤ *Woo Lae Ok*
118-1, Chugyo-dong
Chung-gu, Seoul
Tel: (02) 265-0151
• The specialty of this restaurant is *naengmyon*, buckwheat noodles in a cold broth of vinegar and mustard.

➤ *Ham Hung Myon Ok*
1-12 Ogum-dong
Songp'a-gu, Seoul
Tel: (02) 404-1919
• Go here for a variety of *kalbi* short ribs and *naengmyon*.

➤ *Chonju Chung-ang Hoegwan*
90-1, Pukch'ang-dong
Chung-gu, Seoul
Tel: (02) 754-7789
• The specialty of this restaurant is *pibimpap*, selections of meat, egg, vegetables, and bean sprouts over rice served with a spicy chili paste.

➤ *It'aewon Garden*
112-5, It'aewon-dong
Yongsan-gu, Seoul
Tel: (02) 797-1474
• Located in a popular tourist area, this restaurant serves a wide variety of *kalbi* and *pulgogi* dishes.

WHAT TO SEE AND DO

➤ *Kyongju National Museum*
This is one of South Korea's finest museums, housing more than 12,000 exhibits from the Shilla era. Closed on Monday. Located at 76, Inwang-dong, Kyongju, Kyongsangbuk-do.

➤ *Kyongbokkung Palace*
This houses the main branch of the National Museum, which has a collection of more than 120,000 Korean artifacts. It is closed on Mondays. The adjoining National Folklore Museum, which has

more than 10,000 folk-culture items, is closed on Tuesdays. Both are located at 1, Sejongno, Chongno-gu, Seoul.

➤ *Mt. Puk'ansan National Park*
Located thirty minutes out of Seoul, this is a great place to hike and rock climb.

➤ *National Museum of Contemporary Art*
Displays include more than 3,000 works of modern art. Closed on Mondays. Located at 159-1, Makkye-dong, Kwach'on, Kyonggi-do.

➤ *Korean Folk Village*
This living museum near Suwon recreates the Korean lifestyle of several centuries ago. It consists of houses, restaurants, and an amphitheater for music and folk-dance performances.

➤ *P'anmunjom*
Located inside the Demilitarized Zone between North and South Korea, this is the site of the armistice negotiations that ended the Korean War in 1953. Full-day tours from Seoul, which include an escorted trip to Freedom House for a view of North Korea, operate Monday through Friday.

Temples and Cathedrals

TEMPLE ETIQUETTE

➤ Remove your shoes when you enter temple buildings, but keep them on for Christian churches, as you would in the West.

➤ When entering a temple or church, cover your shoulders and your legs at least to the knee.

WORTH VISITING

➤ *Kyongguk-sa Temple*
This is a Buddhist temple in the north of Seoul near Chongnung Valley.

➤ *Chogyesa Temple*
Located in Chongno-gu, Seoul, this busy temple within the old city walls is the site of the Lantern Festival in spring, held in celebration of Buddha's Birthday.

USEFUL KOREAN PHRASES

English	Korean	Pronunciation
Good morning, afternoon, evening (formal)	Annyong hashimnikka	Ahn-nyong hashim-ni-kka
Good morning, afternoon, evening (informal)	Annyong haseyo	Ahn-nyong hah-seh-yo
Goodbye	Annyonghi gaseyo	Ahn-nyong-hi ga-seh-yo
Thank you	Kamsa hamnida	Kahm-sah hahm-ni-dah
You're welcome	Ch'onmaneyo	Chon-mahn-eh-yo
Excuse me	Shil-lye hamnida	Shil-yeah hahm-ni-dah
I am sorry	Mian hamnida	Mi-ahn hahm-ni-dah
Yes	Ne	Neh
No	Aniyo	Ah-ni-yo
I understand	Alget sumnida	Ahl-get sum-ni-dah
I don't understand	Moruget sumnida	Maw-roo-get sum-ni-dah
How much?	Olma yimnikka?	Uhlmah yim-ni-kkah?

Korea's official written system, *hangul*, is a phonetic alphabet. You may also see Chinese characters used.

➤ *Pong-unsa Temple*
This Buddhist temple in Yong-dong in the southern part of Seoul is known for its four temple guardian statues.

➤ *Myong-dong Catholic Cathedral*
Located in the Myong-dong area of downtown Seoul, this is South Korea's oldest Catholic church.

SHOPPING

Seoul has a number of good department stores and boutiques selling high-priced goods, as well as a variety of large outdoor markets and souvenir shops. The It'aewon area, in particular, has just about everything you can think of at prices that are still a bargain.

Shopping Tips

➤ English is spoken in most major department stores and shopping areas.

➤ Department stores use a fixed-price system, but expect to bargain at most shops and shopping areas.

➤ If you are having clothes made for you, try them on before you make your final payment, since alterations are best negotiated on the spot. Tailor-made clothing can be put together nearly overnight. Some of the more popular tailors, who are used to serving tourists on short stays, are located in the It'aewon area of Seoul.

➤ Popular South Korean buys include leather jackets and coats, eel-skin accessories, and light-green celadon pottery.

➤ Gemstones indigenous to South Korea include smoky topaz, amethyst, and white jade. Ask for a certificate of authenticity.

➤ Antique items cannot be exported without permission, but there is no paperwork necessary for antique reproductions, some of which are inexpensive and quite nicely done.

➤ Save your receipts. The National Tourist Board will respond to shopping complaints if you can show your receipts.

Markets

➤ *It'aewon*
Most hotels offer free, frequent shuttles to It'aewon, Seoul's most popular tourist shopping area. Western fast-food eateries abound. English is spoken here.

➤ *Tongdaemun Market (East Gate Market)*
This is South Korea's largest, most colorful marketplace. It is closed on the first and third Sundays of the month.

➤ *Namdaemun Market (South Gate Market)*
The winding streets of this market are jam-packed with everyday merchandise. Nandaemun is known for bargain clothing. It is closed on Sundays.

➤ *Insa-dong*
An artists' district, Insa-dong is dotted with bookstores and art galleries. It is also referred to as a "street museum" for its many antique shops. Most shops are closed on Sundays.

➤ *Myong-dong*
This is Seoul's major downtown shopping district for high-quality clothes and shoes.

➤ *Changan-dong Antique Market*
This is a large antique market in eastern Seoul consisting of about 150 shops chock full of old Korean pottery, furniture, and curios. It is closed on Sundays.

➤ *Kyong-dong Market*
This market near Chegi-dong Station in eastern Seoul has many Oriental medicine shops.

➤ *Yongsan Electronics Market*
Some 2,700 shops make this South Korea's largest electronics market. It is closed on the first and third Sundays of each month.

Final Thoughts

A 1995 radio show in California about work ethics and situations presented to its listeners the case of a successful executive woman who was under consideration for an expatriate assignment in Asia. There was considerable resistance to this posting from clients and colleagues overseas, although the woman had proven herself in other regions of the world. The question put to the radio audience was simple: with all your key overseas associates and customers resisting your move, would you nevertheless promote this woman into a position where she would have to daily command their respect?

This woman's situation and the dilemma facing her boss are fairly typical. Women in U.S. firms are only rarely given overseas assignments. Worldwide, in fact, women hold around 3 percent of all international management positions. This circumstance not only hinders the business success of American firms abroad, in Europe as well as in Asia, but it also limits opportunities for women to succeed at home. After all, a multinational company would naturally prefer that its most senior staff have abundant overseas experience. Excluded from that experience, women are excluded from promotions and power.

Nancy Adler, writing in *HR Magazine*, attributes the shortage of women managers overseas to three main factors:

➢ The assumption that women simply do not want to be international managers because of work/family conflicts.

➢ The outright refusal of some companies to send women abroad, owing to fears about their competence or their physical safety.

> ➤ The not entirely mistaken belief that many foreigners are prejudiced against women expatriate managers.

Adler's survey of more than 1,000 graduating M.B.A.'s reveals that female and male M.B.A.'s are equally interested in pursuing international careers. Another survey of women expatriates concluded that more than half of these international managers felt that being female was more of an advantage overseas than a disadvantage.[1]

Clearly, the Western corporate world is neither satisfying women's expectations nor assessing their overseas situations accurately. Clearly, companies need to develop a new corporate attitude toward sending women managers on international assignments.

There are many advantages to sending women overseas. Since there aren't many women in overseas executive assignments, those women who *are* there stand out and are remembered by their associates and partners. Women also have an advantage when it comes to interpersonal skills. Compared to foreign, male managers, local male employees find women easier to talk to on a wider range of topics. Women receive special treatment not often offered to men, which may help break the ice of a new business relationship or set a standard of civility and mutual respect. Women also benefit from a "halo effect": Since so few women are sent abroad the local business community assumes the woman is undoubtedly the foreign company's very best manager.

Despite the advantages of their gender, however, most U.S. professional women state that when they work overseas they are seen first as American and second as female, regardless of how the country treats their local women. Gender for them is not so big an issue.[2]

It turns out, in fact, that most of the problems for women managers overseas are the result of attitudes and actions on the part of their home companies. The home company's first mistake is failing to consider sending a woman overseas at all. The second error lies in failing to strongly endorse and support her when she is sent; lacking a supportive environment at start-up, the woman is set up to fail, and the firm's clients infer a lack of commitment. The third mistake is made when the company limits the woman's power while she is overseas: a manager who always has to call back to the home office or who has senior people constantly flying in to "check up" on things after a while loses the confidence of her clients.

But the future is getting brighter for women. On the radio program mentioned above, almost all the people who called in said that the woman should indeed be given the new position in Asia. Many emphasized that professional strengths overcome any cultural bias. Others spoke about how the world is changing, how the older Asian men who run many of Asia's top corporations are retiring and being replaced by more modern, forward-thinking leaders.

As Asia changes, we can only hope that our own corporations at home improve their policies and attitudes as well. The goal? To be ready and willing to invest in the wealth of opportunities that Asia presents with the very best human capital our society has to offer, regardless of gender.

Appendixes

Appendix 1

PRESENTATIONS

The business presentation is an excellent tool for positioning your products or your firm's goals with your Asian business peers. If you are selling, you can use your presentation to demonstrate the value of your company and your product line. If you are the customer, you can use it to delineate your business goals and objectives. Giving a presentation may be the first interaction you will have with your Asian counterparts, so remember that this first impression can make or break your firm.

Presentation formats and styles differ from country to country. Even the best presenters may have some trouble positioning their companies with Asian firms, since techniques that are effective at home may not be effective in Asia.

Presentation Pitfalls

➢ The presenter is so informed about his or her company's products that he or she speaks rapidly and uses industry-specific slang, which may be untranslatable.

➢ The presenter may free associate or present stimulating new ideas during the presentation that deviate from the agenda and expectations of the audience.

➢ The presenter may become very intense or excited about his or her products and give an emotion-tinged presentation.

➤ The presenter may interact with the audience to prompt them for questions or get them excited.

The Asian View

While you may be used to interacting with your audience and making them respond to your very visible enthusiasm, such techniques—essential in your country—should generally be avoided in Asia. Why?

➤ Asians are accustomed to following an agenda and do not expect any surprises or new concepts. Your Asian business peers are ready, when you give your presentation, to respond to your agenda. New ideas may first need to be reviewed by the firm's executive members before a response can be made.

➤ Industry jargon is not easily translated into other languages, so if it is unfamiliar to your Asian business contacts, your concepts may be lost or misunderstood.

➤ Many Asians speak and understand English but will become lost if the speaker is talking too rapidly. This can happen very quickly if you are presenting a complicated topic or technical concept.

➤ Asians, in general, do not show emotion during business meetings. Any emotion, even overenthusiasm, may therefore be misinterpreted or detract from the impact of your presentation.

➤ Asians generally do not ask questions in a group setting, even if questions are asked for. However, they will often share their thoughts and questions in smaller settings, particularly one-on-one.

Presentation Pointers

Here are some tips and pointers we have learned from seasoned business-people on giving a presentation to an Asian group:

SPEECH

➤ Keep your presentation short and to the point.

➤ Speak slowly and clearly so your words can be easily understood.

➤ Avoid industry slang that may not be understood, such as "the Net."

➤ Avoid negative questions or statements such as "This is not red, is it?" —these can be very confusing to non-native English speakers.

➤ Do not use jokes; humor does not translate well across cultures.

➤ Avoid idioms like "in the ballpark" or "water under the bridge" since they are not always understood and could be translated literally.

➤ Keep the tone of your voice at a moderate level. Loud or expressive speech will detract from your presentation and make you appear too emotional. As a woman especially you have to guard against falling into the Asian female stereotype.

GESTURES

➤ Limit your use of direct eye contact, which might be considered rude or aggressive. Instead, keep your eyes on your audience's ties or ears.

➤ Minimize pacing. Do not, for example, walk up to a person and peer into his or her eyes to make a point.

➤ Keep your hands relaxed and visible to your audience. Do not put them behind your back or in your pockets.

➤ Limit your hand and arm movements. Try not to fling your arms around to express yourself, since your Asian peers will be watching your limbs rather than listening to your words. Waving your hands and arms around may also be interpreted as being aggressive.

➤ Keep your facial expression neutrally pleasant. A smile, for example, may indicate anything from anger to sorrow or happiness.

MATERIALS

➤ Use demonstration props wherever you can to highlight your points or company products and services. Props will help you keep your words to a minimum. Point at the product features as you describe them.

➤ Provide a copy of everything for your audience. English is generally easier for Asians to understand when it is written down.

➤ If possible, have your key documents translated into the native language, since this will make it much easier for your Asian counterparts to review your presentation after you have left.

➤ Be sure your presentation tapes are the right format for the country. Singapore and Hongkong use PAL. Taiwan and South Korea use VHS, the same as the United States.

STRATEGIES FOR SUCCESS

➤ Dress conservatively.

➤ To create a good first impression, present yourself as sincere, confident, and professional. Make yourself warm, compromising, and easy to work with. If Asians think you have primarily profit in mind they will consider you insincere or aggressive.

➤ Keep a calm, comfortable stance to avoid appearing overbearing.

➤ Open your presentation by thanking your guests for taking time from their busy schedules to attend the meeting.

➤ State the main points of your presentation at the beginning and then repeat them in your wrap-up.

➤ Stick to the agenda. Surprises are not expected or welcomed.

➤ Because your Asian counterparts will often smile and agree during the presentation in an effort to maintain harmony, you should frame questions so they need to be answered in sentences rather than by a yes or no. This will help ensure that your point has been understood.

➤ Listen actively. You will be more effective if you listen to and question your counterparts rather than simply respond.

➤ Avoid disagreement. Do not encourage debate or respond negatively to questions. If someone makes a point you do not agree with, remain calm and acknowledge it. Probe for a better understanding of what the point is and plan to address it in a one-on-one situation.

➤ After your presentation there may be little response, since presentations in Asia are usually not interactive. Set up opportunities for your counterparts to ask questions in a smaller, more comfortable setting.

➤ Do not push for a decision on the spot. Many times your counterparts will need to discuss the points internally before making a decision.

Appendix 2

SAFETY

No matter where you travel in the world, there are risks to your security and well-being. Females account for over 40 percent of the total number of world travelers, and this number is growing. Generally smaller and physically weaker than men, women are often viewed as being ill equipped to protect themselves during robberies or assaults. Consequently, it pays to be aware of practical measures you can take to help ensure your safety.

Asia is a relatively safe area in which to travel, but no place is completely problem free. Of the Four Tigers, Singapore is considered the safest destination, and Hong Kong the least safe. Taiwan and Korea fall somewhere in between the two.

General Tips and Pointers

➢ If you look confident, walk assertively, and act like you know where you are going, you will be less likely to be targeted. Tourists who look like tourists are more likely to be approached than people who blend in with the locals.

➢ It is unusual for Asians to start up a conversation with a stranger. If someone does so with you and acts very friendly, he may just be curious or trying to be helpful. Remain alert, however, in case he has other intentions.

➢ If someone who follows you into an elevator looks suspicious, walk out. If you are already in an elevator, hop off at the next floor and wait for another elevator car.

➤ If you want to sightsee at night, go with a colleague or take a reputable tour. It is usually not a good idea to wander around at night on your own no matter how safe the area may seem to be.

➤ Sling your handbag across the front of your body to prevent it from being grabbed off your shoulder from behind. Don't put it around your neck so you won't get choked if someone tries to nab it. It is best to keep your bag close to your body and under your coat, if you are wearing one.

➤ Keep your wallet in a compartment in your bag so it is not visible on top of your purse. Keep your purse closed unless you are getting something out of it.

➤ Keep the strap of your handbag wrapped around your leg during meals in restaurants to avoid having it stolen by a passerby.

➤ Don't let others know that you are traveling alone.

➤ Consider carrying a whistle, pepper spray, or mace for protection.

➤ Wear sensible shoes so that you can move quickly if someone approaches you.

➤ Use automatic teller machines or public telephones in a well-lighted area where there is some pedestrian traffic. If possible, have someone accompany you.

➤ Try to avoid walking through underground passages or tunnels if there is no one else around or at night.

➤ Most of your business will probably be in the larger cities. Keep to the crowded, well-lit areas and avoid quiet, dark streets.

Airport

➤ If you have an ID tag on your luggage, use your work address and phone number to avoid revealing any personal information.

➤ Never leave your luggage unattended. Airports and bus stations are prime target areas for luggage switches or thievery.

➤ Distinguish your luggage with visible identity tags.

➤ Be attentive when you are exchanging money at airports. Keep a close watch on your luggage. Do not flash your cash.

Transportation

➤ Use the hotel taxi and bus services rather than wandering the streets trying to find a cab. Hotel staff will help you, but if you are on your own make sure the taxi is marked with a company logo and license and that there is a meter and driver ID in the car.

➤ Take your taxi cards and your hotel card with you wherever you go. If you need transportation from a restaurant, you want to be able to make sure you can call a reputable taxi. The hotel card has the correct address of your hotel in the local language so that you will be sure to get a direct route back.

➤ The trains in Asia are often very crowded. If you are on the train, keep your purse close to your body to avoid pickpockets. Keep your cash in an inside pocket of your skirt, pants, or jacket.

➤ If you are taking the train or subway at night, sit in a car where there are people. If possible, avoid late-night rides.

➤ When you are waiting for a train, stand near other people, not off alone by yourself. At night, keep near the well-lit areas.

Hotels

➤ Stay in well-known hotels in central, populated areas. Hotels off the beaten path are less likely to have good tourist accommodations and amenities. Tourist hotels usually make a strong attempt to measure up to Western expectations, and, in many cases, may even exceed them. Major Western hotel chains are usually in central locations and can offer uniformed, around-the-clock personnel, up-to-date lock systems, clean rooms, and good fire-escape routes.

➤ Keep all your valuables in the hotel safe or in the small safe you will find in many Asian hotel rooms.

> Keep your passport on your person or locked in the hotel safe. Make a copy of your passport so you have the information at hand for the embassy if it is lost or stolen.

> Be sure the person who escorts you and enters your room during check-in is part of the hotel staff. Staff should be wearing uniforms.

> Meet guests in the lobby of the hotel rather than giving them your room number to come up and fetch you.

> Check the locks on your doors and windows when you enter your room. Check that local emergency numbers are posted by the telephone. Make sure you have a fire-escape route.

> Hotel personnel are instructed not to give out room numbers. If you find that your room number has been given out to someone, request a change of rooms and notify the front desk that your room number must be kept private. Be particularly watchful at check-in; instruct the clerk not to say your room number out loud when handing you your key.

> Most large tourist hotels have programmable card keys that are reprogrammed after each guest to ensure security. Card keys do not have the room number on them. If you are staying in an older hotel, you may be given a traditional room key with the number on it. Keep the key with you.

> Select a room that faces an interior courtyard rather than the street, where others can monitor your coming and going.

> Double lock your door when you are taking a shower or retiring. These are the most likely times for someone to try to enter your room.

> If you order room service, don't put your tray outside your door. Someone could deduce that you are alone by the number of dishes.

Appendix 3

GOLF

Golf is often included in the business program in Asia, where it is still mostly a man's game. But golf is no longer only for men, so if you enjoy the game, take advantage of the opportunities to play alongside your host and male colleagues. You will certainly be noticed, and it is an excellent way for you to build your business relationships. When you play in Asia, you need to have a good understanding of the rules of the game as well as course etiquette.

Most Asian golf courses are private and require membership or an invitation from a member, so it will be difficult for you to play if you have not been invited as a guest. Many clubs also require visitors to hold a handicap or proficiency certificate from a recognized club. Some of the major hotels offer golf packages and some courses may offer non-member days. In general, it is best to call individual clubs for details or make reservations through your local offices, travel agent, or hotel in advance of your trip. Tee times are hard to secure, especially on weekends, and the fees will probably be higher than what you would pay at home. You will be required to use a cart, a caddy, or both. If you travel to Asia frequently, consider getting one of the overseas corporate memberships available through some golf resorts. These memberships will enable you to play on affiliated courses throughout the region.

The listings here are based on information provided by the clubs themselves. Where available we have tried to include pars and course lengths, general fees, and any restrictions, as well as information about notable other facilities that may be available to you.

Hong Kong

Hong Kong has three participating golf clubs comprising four golf courses. Golf is still a members-only activity in Hong Kong. Some clubs allow members to bring guests or overseas visitors to use the club and facilities during the week. One sports and recreation tour available offers visitors green fees for eighteen holes of golf, swimming, or sauna and a Western-style lunch, plus transportation by air-conditioned bus and guide service. Usual tour days are Tuesdays and Fridays for about HK$1,100. You can make arrangements through your travel agent or hotel tour desks.

➤ *Clearwater Bay Golf and Country Club*
Lot #227 in D.D. 241, Po Toi O, Sai Kung
New Territories, Hong Kong
Tel: 2719-5936
• 18 holes, par 70
• Guest green fees: HK$1,100 for 18 holes
• Club rental fees: HK$250 for 18 holes
• Electric cart rental fee : HK$240 for 18 holes

➤ *Discovery Bay Golf Course*
Valley Road, Discovery Bay
Lantau Island, Hong Kong
Tel: 2987-7271
Fax: 2987-5900
• 27 holes (Jade 9, Ruby 9, Diamond 9)
• Pars: Diamond/Jade par, 71; Jade/Ruby, par 70; Ruby/Diamond, par 70
• Guest green fees: HK$700 for 18 holes
• Club rental fees: HK$150 for 18 holes
• Electric cart fee: HK$180 for 18 holes

➤ *The Royal Hong Kong Golf Club, Fanling*
P.O. Box 1, Shek Wu Hui Post Office
New Territories, Hong Kong
Tel: 2670-1211
Fax: 2679-5183
• Three 18-hole golf courses (Old, New, Eden)
• Ladies pars: Old, par 72; New, par 71; Eden, par 71

- Guest green fees: HK$1,100 for 18 holes
- Guests can play on weekdays only (no public holidays) on a first-come first-served basis
- Club rental fees: $250 for 18 holes, hand cart included
- Caddy (optional) fees: HK$110 for a bag carrier, $155 for a regular caddy, $200 for a senior caddy

➢ *The Royal Hong Kong Golf Club*
19 Island Road, Deepwater Bay
Hong Kong
Tel: 2812-7070
Fax: 2812-7111

- Guest green fees: HK$350 for 18 holes, HK$500 for 36 holes
- Guests can play on weekdays only (no public holidays) on a first-come, first-served basis
- Ladies par: front 9, par 28; back 9, par 28
- Caddy (optional) fees: HK$45 for 9 holes, HK$80 for 18 holes, HK$160 for 36 holes

➢ *Chung Shan Hot Spring Golf Club Hotel*
Located across Hong Kong Harbor in Guangdong Province, China

- A day visa is required, which you can secure in Hong Kong; ask your hotel to help with reservations
- 18 holes, par 71
- Elegant resort with 7 ponds

FOR FURTHER INFORMATION

➢ *The Golf Association of Hong Kong*
GPO Box 9978
#110, Yu To Sang Building
37 Queens Road Central
Hong Kong

Taiwan

There are twenty-five golf courses open to visitors in Taiwan, about half of which are within easy driving distance of Taipei. Make arrangements through your hotel or through the Taiwan Tourist Bureau before you leave home. Caddies and rental equipment are available.

➤ *The Taiwan Golf and Country Club*
2 Yoo-che Li
Tamsui, Taipei County
Tel: (02) 621-2211
- 18 holes, 7,015 yards, par 72; 9 holes, 3011 yards, par 35
- Guest fees: weekdays, NT$1,800; weekends, holidays, NT$2,100
- Caddy fees: NT$700

➤ *Chang Gung Golf and Country Club*
23-4 Chiu-lu Village
Kuei-shan, Taoyuan County
Tel: (03) 329-6354
- 18 holes, 7,105 yds, par 72
- Guest fees: weekdays, NT$2,000; weekends, holidays, NT$2,000
- Caddy fees: NT$580

➤ *The New Tamsui Gold Club*
300 Pa-shih Road
Tamsui, Taipei County
Tel: (02) 809-2208 or (02) 809-2466
- 18 holes, 6,620 yards, par 72
- Guest fees: weekdays, NT$1,200; weekends, holidays: NT $1,800
- Caddy fees: NT$500

➤ *Far Eastern Golf Club*
19 Nanya South Road
Panchiao, Taipei County
Tel: (02) 954-9048 or (02) 958-5622
- 18 holes, 6,301 yards, par 70
- Guest fees: weekdays, NT$525; weekends, holidays, NT$840
- Caddy fees: NT$390–450

➤ *Linkou International Golf and Country Club*
50-1 Hupei Village
Linkou, Taipei County
Tel: (02) 601-1211
- 18 holes, 6,150 yards, par 72; 9 holes, 2,910 yards, par 36
- Guest fees: weekdays, NT$1,500; weekends, holidays, NT $2,000
- Caddy fees: NT$520–550

➤ *Taipei Golf Club*
P.O. Box 15
Lu-chu, Taoyuan County
Tel: (03) 324-1311 or (03) 324-4956
- South course: 18 holes, 6,420 yards, par 72; North course: 18 holes, 6,611 yards, par 72
- Guest fees: Wednesdays, NT$850; weekdays, NT$1,250; weekends, holidays, NT$1,650
- Caddy fees: NT$400–550

➤ *Marshall Golf Country Club*
33, Ying Pang Kung, Wu-Fu Village
Lu Chu, Taoyuan County
Tel: (03) 322-1786
- 18 holes, 7,000 yards, par 72
- Guest fees: weekdays, NT $1,250; weekends, holidays, NT$1,650
- Caddy fees: NT$500

➤ *Taoyuan Golf Club*
39 Chiutsuolio
Chiulung Village
Lungtan, Taoyuan County
Tel: (03) 470-1616 or (03) 489-4349
- 18 holes, 7,450 yards, par 74
- Guest fees: weekdays, NT$1,200; weekends, holidays, NT$1,800
- Caddy fees: NT$510–580

➤ *Taichung Golf and Country Club*
20 Tungshan Road, Hengshan Village
Taya, Taichung County
Tel: (045) 665-1302
- 18 holes, 6,991 yards, par 72
- Guest fees: weekdays, NT $1,000; weekends, holidays, NT$1,800
- Caddy fees: NT$400–500

➤ *Woo Fong Golf Club*
648 Feng-ku Road, Feng-ku Village
Wu Feng, Taichung County
Tel: (04) 330-1199
- 18 holes, 6,723 yards, par 72

- Guest fees: weekdays, NT$1,000; weekends, holidays, NT $1,600
- Caddy fees: NT$370–450

➤ *Chang Hwa Golf Club*
101 Lane 2, Ta Pu Road
Chang Hua
Tel: (047) 252-603 or (047) 243-322
- 18 holes, par 72
- Guest fees: weekdays, NT$1,000; weekends, holidays, NT$1,400
- Caddy fees: NT$450–500

➤ *Tainan Golf Club*
100 Chiao-Keng, Li
Hsin-hwa, Tainan County
Tel: (06) 590-1666
- 18 holes, 6,849 yards, par 72
- Guest fees: weekdays, NT$700; weekends, holidays, NT$1,400
- Caddy fees: NT$460

➤ *Hsin Yee Golf Club*
1 Hsin Yi Road, Chung Ling Village
Ta-shu, Kaohsiung County
Tel: (07) 656-3210
- 18 holes, 7,429 yards, par 72
- Guest fees: weekdays, NT$1,600; weekends, holidays, NT$2,000
- Caddy fees: NT$500

➤ *Eagle Golf Course*
14, 14 Ling, Nan Keng, Sen-shui Village
Lungtan, Taoyuan County
Tel: (03) 471-8305
- 18 holes, par 72
- Swimming pool, tennis courts, fitness center
- 20 minutes from CKS International Airport
- Inquire about fees

FOR FURTHER INFORMATION

➤ *ROC Golf Association*
MS, Lane 187, Tunhua South Road
Section 1, Taipei

Singapore

Golf is popular in Singapore. Hours are usually from 7 A.M. to 7 P.M. Some clubs offer night golf until 11 P.M. Weekend tee times are hard to obtain, since these are mostly reserved for members. Fees range from S$50 to S$220. Non-members may be allowed to play for a special fee. Contact the club for details. Driving ranges are also available where you can practice your drives for as little as S$3 for 48 balls.

➤ *Changi Golf Club*
   20 Netheravon Road
   Singapore
   Tel: 545-5133
   Fax: 545-2531
   • Par 68
   • Green fees: S$50
   • Caddy fees: S$14–19

➤ *Singapore Island Country Club*
   180 Island Club Road
   Singapore
   Tel: 459-2222
   Fax: 458-3796
   • Two 18-hole, par-72 courses
   • Green fees: S$130 (weekdays only)
   • Caddy fees: S$18–25

➤ *Sentosa Golf Club*
   Sentosa Island
   Singapore
   Tel: 275-0022
   Fax: 275-0005
   • Par 72, 7,100 yards
   • Green fees: weekdays, $S60; weekends, S$120
   • Clubs rental: S$15

➤ *Warren Golf Course*
   Folkestone Road
   Singapore
   Tel: 777-6533
   Fax: 778-5502

- 9 holes, par 70
- Driving range
- Green fees: weekday, S$50
- Caddy fees: S$18–25

➤ *Sembawang Country Club (c/o Sembawang Airbase)*
17km Sembawang Road
Singapore
Tel: 481-4745 or 257-0642
Fax: 752-0446
- 18 holes, par 70
- Green fees: Tuesdays–Fridays only, S$80
- Caddy fees: S$15–20
- Driving range

➤ *Raffles Country Club*
450 Jalan Ahmad Ibrahim
Singapore
Tel: 861-7655
Fax: 861-5563
- Two 18-hole courses (pars 69 and 71)
- Green fees: weekdays, S$100; weekends, S$160
- Driving range

➤ *Seletar Country Club*
Seletar Airbase
3 Parklane
Singapore
Tel: 481-4745
Fax: 481-3000
- 9 holes, par 70
- Green fees: Tuesday–Friday only, S$80
- Caddy fees: S$15–20
- Driving range

➤ *Keppel Club*
Bukit Chermin
Singapore
Tel: 273-5522
Fax: 272-1563
- 18 holes, par 72

- Green fees: weekdays, S$90; weekends, S$150
- Caddy fees: S$25 for 18 holes
- Driving range

DRIVING RANGES

➤ *Marina Bay Golf and Country Club*
Marina South
Singapore
Tel: 221-2811
Fax: 221-7171
- 3 high-level driving ranges, 150 bays, 230-meter fairway, 9-hole putting green
- Fee: 100 balls, S$9
- Day membership available

➤ *Parkland Driving Range*
920 East Coast Parkway
Singapore
Tel: 440-6726
Fax: 345-2138
- 60 bays, 200-meter range
- Fee: 95 balls before 3:30 P.M., S$5; S$6 after 3:30 P.M. and weekends

FOR FURTHER INFORMATION

➤ *The Singapore Golf Association*
c/o C.L. Loong and Co.
4 Battery Road #12-00
Bank of China Building
Singapore

South Korea

Golf is also very popular in Korea. There are more than sixty courses, at least a third of which are near Seoul and easily accessible by car. Tourist hotels, especially in resort areas, can arrange for you to play. Many courses offer lodging houses, youth hostels, tennis courts, and swimming pools. Some are even equipped with lights for night play.

In general, there are two kinds of golf courses in terms of bookings. At some courses only members are allowed to book on Saturday and Sunday afternoons and holidays; non-members are allowed to book on weekdays or can play on a Sunday if they are with a member or a member has booked them as a guest. At other courses (usually higher grade) the policy is members-only play all week; a non-member can play if he or she is included in a member foursome, but this is sometimes more difficult to arrange.

Reservations are a must and should be made one to two weeks in advance. Individual course fees are not given in the listings below, but in general green fees for non-members are around KW45,000 on weekdays and KW49,000 on weekends. Additional fees include a tip for caddy service of KW20,000, clubs rental of KW15,000 for a full set, and shoe rental of KW3,000. There are three classes of caddies, but all provide the same service (the different fees, varying at most only $20–25, reflect the caddy's level of seniority and expertise). If you bring your own clubs, you must declare them at customs when entering South Korea. Hours are usually between sunrise and sunset, though some courses are open at night.

Courses listed here are all in the Seoul metropolitan or surrounding areas.

SEOUL

➤ *Namsongdae*
419, Changji-dong, Songp'a-gu
Tel: (02) 403-0071
• 18 holes

➤ *Taenung (Yuksa)*
230-30, Kongnung-dong, Nowon-gu
Tel: (02) 972-2111
• 18 holes

INCH'ON

➤ *Inch'on Kukche*
177-1 Kyongso-myon, So-gu
Tel: (032) 514-9991 or (02) 783-7091
• 18 holes

KYONGGI-DO

➤ *Anyang*
1, Pugok-dong, Kunp'o-shi
Tel: (02) 866-1414 or (0343) 62-0051
• 18 holes

➤ *Gold*
San 18, Komak-ri, Kihung-up, Yongin-gun
Tel: (02) 777-2160 or (0331) 283-8111
• 36 holes

➤ *Taegwang*
San 66, Shingal-ri, Kihung-up, Yongin-gun
Tel: (0331) 281-7111
• 27 holes

➤ *Hansung*
32-1, Pojong-ri, Kusong-myon, Yongin-gun
Tel: (02) 236-4511 or (0331) 284-3831
• 27 holes

➤ *Hanyang*
San 38-23, Wondang-dong, Koyang-shi
Tel: (02) 357-0901
• 36 holes

➤ *Cheil*
San 587, Pugok-dong, Ansan-shi
Tel: (02) 233-6202 or (0345) 405-1212
• 27 holes

➤ *Yong-in Plaza*
San 57, Pongmu-ri, Namsa-myon, Yongin-gun
Tel: (02) 745-5311 or (0335) 32-6761
• 36 holes

➤ *Suwon*
313, Kugal-ri, Kihung-up, Yongin-gun
Tel: (02) 233-5597 or (0331) 281-6613
• 27 holes

➤ *Yeojoo (Yochu)*
35-10, Wolsong-ri, Yoju-up, Yoju-gun
Tel: (02) 752-3489 or (0337) 82-5881
• 27 holes

➤ *Jungbu (Chungbu)*
28-1, Konjiam-ri, Shilch'on-myon, Kwangju-gun
Tel: (02) 745-8338 or (0347) 62-6588
• 18 holes

➤ *New Seoul*
1, Sam-ri, Kwangju-up, Kwangju-gun
Tel: (02) 745-5778 or (0347) 62-5672
• 36 holes

➤ *Yangji*
34-1, Namgok-ri, Naesa-myon, Yongin-gun
Tel: (02) 744-2001 or (0335) 33-2001
• 27 holes

➤ *Duckpyung*
53-3, Maegok-ri, Hobop-myon, Ich'on-gun
Tel: (0336) 638-9626
• 18 holes

➤ *Dong Seoul*
260-1, Kam 2-dong, Hanam-shi
Tel: (02) 470-2141
• 18 holes

➤ *Royal*
555, Mansong-ri, Chunae-myon, Yangju-gun
Tel: (02) 739-3971 or (0351) 40-1515
• 18 holes

FOR FURTHER INFORMATION

➤ *The Korea Golf Association*
Room 18, 13th Floor
Manhattan Building
36-2, Youido-dong
Seoul, South Korea

Notes

CHAPTER 2: DOING BUSINESS NINE TO FIVE

1 John King Fairbank, *China: A New History* (Cambridge, Mass: Belknap Press, Harvard University Press, 1992).

CHAPTER 4: SEXUAL HARASSMENT

1 Anita Cava and Don Mayer, "Gender Discrimination Abroad," *Business and Economic Review*, Oct.–Dec. 1993, pp. 13–16.

CHAPTER 5: DINING

1 Daniel Reid, *Taiwan* (Singapore: APA Publications, 1989).

CHAPTER 6: HONG KONG

1 Corinna T. de Leon and Suk-ching Ho, "Hong Kong: The Third Identity of Modern Chinese Women: Women Managers in Hong Kong." In Nancy J. Adler and Dafna N. Izraeli, eds., *Competitive Frontiers: Women Managers in a Global Economy* (Cambridge, Mass: Blackwell Publishers, 1994).

2 P. Kirkbride and E. Chan, "Emigration from Hong Kong," *Human Resources Journal,* Vol. 4, No. 2 (1988), pp. 5–17

3 *Ming Pao Daily*, "Emigration of Managerial Personnel Will Peak Again After a Temporary Levelling Off," September 26, 1990.

4 Dolecheck and Dolecheck, "Discrimination of Women in the Work Place," *Human Resources Journal*, Vol. 3, No. 1 (1987), pp. 37–44.

5   *Hong Kong Standard*, "Hong Kong a Haven for Working Women," November 28, 1990.

CHAPTER 7: TAIWAN

1   Kathleen S. Crittenden, "Asian Self-effacement or Feminine Modesty? Attributional Patterns of Women University Students in Taiwan," *Gender and Society*, March 1991, pp. 98–117.

2   Michael Tang, "A Survey of Women Managers in Taiwan: Perceptions and Perspectives," *Asia Pacific Journal of Management*, April 1992, pp. 95–105.

3   Kenneth Gannicott, "Women, Wages and Discrimination: Some Evidence from Taiwan," *Economic Development and Cultural Change*, Vol. 34, No. 4 (July 1986), pp. 721–30.

4   Business International Corp., "Taiwan," *Investing, Licensing, and Trading Conditions Abroad*, August 1, 1992.

CHAPTER 8: SINGAPORE

1   Audrey Chan,"Women Managers in Singapore: Citizens for Tomorrow's Economy." In Nancy J. Adler and Dafna N. Izraeli, eds., *Women in Management Worldwide* (Armonk, N.Y.: M. E. Sharpe, 1988), pp. 54–73.

2   Audrey Chan and Jean J. Lee, "Singapore: Women Executives in a Newly Industrialized Economy: The Singapore Scenario." In Adler and Izraeli, *Competitive Frontiers*.

3   Sam Aryee, "Antecedents and Outcomes of Work-Family Conflict among Married Professional Women: Evidence from Singapore," *Human Relations*, Vol. 45, No. 8 (August 1992), pp. 813–37.

CHAPTER 9: SOUTH KOREA

1   Business International Corp., "South Korea's Market Poses Problems, but Offers Rewards," *Business Asia*, December 16, 1991.

FINAL THOUGHTS

1   These surveys and conclusions are discussed in Nancy Adler, *HR Magazine*, "Women Managers in a Global Economy," Vol. 38, No. 9 (September 1993), pp. 52–55.

2   Susana Barciela. "Their Ranks Have Grown, But Women Working Abroad Still Face Hurdles," *Journal of Commerce*, Wednesday, April 13, 1994.

Bibliography

Aryee, Sam. "Antecedents and Outcomes of Work-Family Conflict among Married Professional Women: Evidence from Singapore." *Human Relations*, Vol. 45, No. 8 (August 1992), pp. 813–37.

Axtell, Roger E. *The Do's and Taboos of Hosting International Visitors*. New York: John Wiley and Sons, 1990.

———. *The Do's and Taboos of International Trade*. New York: John Wiley and Sons, 1989.

Brannen, Christalyn, and Tracey Wilen. *Doing Business With Japanese Men: A Woman's Handbook*. Berkeley, Calif.: Stone Bridge Press, 1993.

Business International Corp. "Taiwan." *Investing, Licensing, and Trading Conditions Abroad*, August 1, 1992.

———. "South Korea's Market Poses Problems, but Offers Rewards." *Business Asia*, December 16, 1991.

Cava, Anita, and Don Mayer. "Gender Discrimination Abroad." *Business and Economic Review*, Oct.–Dec. 1993, pp. 13–16.

Chan, Audrey. "Women Managers in Singapore: Citizens for Tomorrow's Economy," In Nancy J. Adler and Dafna N. Izraeli, eds., *Women in Management Worldwide*. Armonk. N.Y.: M.E. Sharpe, 1988.

———, and Jean J. Lee. "Singapore: Women Executives in a Newly Industrialized Economy: The Singapore Scenario." In Nancy J. Adler and Dafna N. Izraeli, eds., *Competitive Frontiers: Women Managers in a Global Economy*. Cambridge, Mass.: Blackwell, 1994.

China External Trade Development Council. *Doing Business with Taiwan ROC*. Taipei: CETRA, 1992.

Crittenden, Kathleen S. "Asian Self-effacement or Feminine Modesty? Attributional Patterns of Women University Students in Taiwan." *Gender and Society*, March 1991, pp. 98–117.

de Leon, Corinna T., and Suk-ching Ho. "Hong Kong: The Third Identity of Modern Chinese Women: Women Managers in Hong Kong." In Nancy J. Adler and Dafna N. Izraeli, eds., *Competitive Frontiers: Women Managers in a Global Economy*, pp. 43–56. Cambridge, Mass.: Blackwell Publishers, 1994.

De Mente, Boye Lafayette. *Chinese Etiquette and Ethics in Business*. Lincolnwood, Ill.: NTC Business Books, NTC Publishing Group, 1989.

———. *Korean Etiquette and Ethics in Business*. 2nd ed. Lincolnwood, Ill.: NTC Business Books, NTC Publishing Group, 1994.

"Demographic Indicators—Taiwan." *Country Profile*, Aug. 10, 1992.

Dolecheck and Dolecheck. "Discrimination of Women in the Work Place." *Human Resources Journal*, Vol. 3, No. 1 (1987).

Dupont, M. Kay. *Business Etiquette and Professionalism: Your Guide to Career Success*. Menlo Park, Calif.: Crisp Publications, 1990.

Elashmawi, Farid, and Philip R. Harris. *Multicultural Management: New Skills for Global Success*. Houston: Gulf Publishing, 1993.

Elegant, Robert. *Pacific Destiny: The Rise of the East*. London: Headline Book Publishing, 1991.

Engholm, Christopher. *When Business East Meets Business West: The Guide to Practice and Protocol in the Pacific Rim*. New York: John Wiley and Sons, 1991.

Fairbank, John King. *China: A New History*. Cambridge, Mass: Belknap Press, Harvard University Press, 1992.

———; Edwin O. Reischauer; and Albert M. Craig. *East Asia: Tradition and Transformation*. Boston: Houghton Mifflin, 1973.

Gannicott, Kenneth. "Women, Wages, and Discrimination: Some Evidence from Taiwan." *Economic Development and Cultural Change*, Vol. 34, No. 4 (July 1986), pp. 721–30.

Gates, Anita. "The Best Hotels for Women." *Working Women Magazine*, Vol. 18, No. 4, April 1993, pp. 77–81.

Hong Kong Standard. "Hong Kong a Haven for Working Women." November 28, 1990.

Keating, John. "More Than Just a Pretty Face." *Asian Business*, November 1989, pp. 56–57.

Kenna, Peggy, and Sondra Lacy. *Business Taiwan: A Practical Guide to Understanding Taiwan's Business Culture*. Lincolnwood, Ill: Passport Books, NTC Publishing Group, 1994.

Kim, H. Edward. *Facts About Korea*. Seoul: Hollym, 1985.

Kirkbride, P., and E. Chan. "Emigration from Hong Kong." *Human Resources Journal*, Vol. 4, No. 2 (1988), pp. 5–17.

Lightle, Juliana, Ph.D., and Betsy Doucet, Esq. *Sexual Harassment in the Workplace: A Guide to Prevention*. Menlo Park, Calif.: Crisp Publications, 1992.

Mahoney, Rhona. "On the Trail of the World's 'Missing Women.'" *Ms. Magazine*, March-April 1992, p. 12.

McCabe, Robert K. *International Herald Tribune Guide to Business Travel in Asia*. Lincolnwood, Ill.: Passport Books, NTC Publishing Group, 1988.

McCleary, K.; P. Weaver; and Li Lan. "Gender Based Differences in Business Travelers' Lodging Preferences."*Cornell Hotel and Restaurant Administration Quarterly*, Vol. 35, No. 2 (April 1994), pp. 51–58.

Millau, Gault. *The Best of Hong Kong*. New York: Simon and Schuster, 1989.

Ming Pao Daily. "Emigration of Managerial Personnel Will Peak Again After a Temporary Levelling Off." September 26, 1990.

Orr, Robert. *Religion in China*. New York: Friendship Press, 1980.

Price Waterhouse, ed. *Doing Business in Taiwan: Information Guide*. Taipei: World Firm Limited, 1991.

―――. *Doing Business in Hong Kong: Information Guide*. Hong Kong: World Firm Limited, 1991.

―――. *Doing Business in Singapore: Information Guide*. Singapore: World Firm Limited, 1991.

Reid, Daniel. *Taiwan*. Singapore: APA Publications, 1989.

Schoenberger, Karl. "Moving between Two Worlds." *Los Angeles Times*, Sunday Final Edition, July 12, 1992.

Steenson, Gary. *Coping with Korea*. New York: Basil Blackwell, 1987.

Tang, Michael T. "A Survey of Women Managers in Taiwan: Perceptions and Perspectives." *Asia Pacific Journal of Management*, April 1992, pp. 95–105.

Tri-Valley Herald, "Taiwanese Women Earning Meager Rights." October 29, 1994, p. B-16.

Wall Street Journal. *Wall Street Journal Guides to Business Travel in the Pacific Rim*. New York and London: Fodor's Travel Publications, 1991.

Webb, Susan L. *Step Forward: Sexual Harassment in the Workplace—What You Need to Know*. New York: Mastermedia, 1991.

Wieman, Earl, ed. *Travel in Taiwan*, Vol. 8, No. 11 (June 1994). Taipei: China Printing Company.

Wilen, Tracey. "Tips from a Woman's Side of the Conference Table," *U.S.-Japan Business Review*, May 6, 1991, p. 6.

———. "The Woman's Advantage." *Upside Magazine*, April 1994, p. 72.

Yager, Jan. *Business Protocol: How to Survive and Succeed in Business.* New York: John Wiley and Sons, 1991.

Index